New African Intellectuals and New African Political Thought
in the Twentieth Century

Waxmann Verlag GmbH
Steinfurter Straße 555, 48159 Münster
info@waxmann.com

Mbukeni Herbert Mnguni (Ed.)

New African Intellectuals and New African Political Thought in the Twentieth Century

Waxmann 2015
Münster • New York

Bibliographic information published by the Deutsche Nationalbibliothek
The Deutsche Nationalbibliothek lists this publication in the
Deutsche Nationalbibliografie; detailed bibliographic data
are available in the Internet at http://dnb.dnb.de

Print-ISBN   978-3-8309-3347-2
E-Book-ISBN 978-3-8309-8347-7

© Waxmann Verlag GmbH, 2015
Münster, Germany

www.waxmann.com
info@waxmann.com

Cover Design: Christian Averbeck, Münster
Cover Picture: © FocalPoint – Fotolia.com
Typesetting: Sven Solterbeck, Münster

Printed on age-resistant paper,
acid-free according to ISO 9706

Printed in Germany

All rights reserved. No part of this publication may be reproduced, stored
in a retrieval system or transmitted in any form or by any means, electronic,
electrostatic, magnetic tape, mechanical, photocopying, recording or
otherwise without permission in writing from the copyright holder.

*This work is dedicated to the
younger generations of African intellectuals*

Contents

Foreword 9
Tunde Adeleke

Acknowledgments 23

Part One

Theorising the Modernist Moment of New African Intellectuals:
From *Imvo Zabantsundu* (1880s) to *Drum* Magazine (1950s) 25
Ntongela Masilela

Part Two

African Intellectuals and the Development of African
Political Thought in the Twentieth Century 111
Mbukeni Herbert Mnguni

Part Three

African Languages: Obstacles to Internationalism
or Additional Wealth for the World? 143
Jabulani S. Maphalala

Index 157

Foreword

Tunde Adeleke[1]

In his "The Problem with Post-Colonial Theory: Re-Theorising African Performance, Orature and Literature in the Age of Globalization and Diaspora Studies," Esiaba Irobi describes Post-Colonial theory as

> a reaction to western imperialist history and intellectual ideology. It is a spirited engagement with the structures of thinking and actions that facilitate the continued subordination, marginalization and exploitation of the intellectual resources and cultural reserves of the previously colonized peoples of the western and non-western worlds. It is also a subtle examination of the many and often conflicted strands that make up the postcolonial situation and identity. It seeks to dismantle the epistemologies of intellectual hegemony cultivated by the west via its academies as well as confront the ex-colonized with the options available for their critical redemption via alternative modes of discourse fashioned by the west.[2]

This definition underscores the counter-hegemonic nature and character of post-colonial theory. Fundamentally, it seeks to engage and deconstruct not just the "epistemology of intellectual hegemony" but also offer the "ex-colonised" options, and an alternative awareness and strategies

---

[1] Tunde Adeleke is a native of Nigeria and presently Professor of History and Director of the African American Studies Program at Iowa State University. He is also affiliated with Iowa State's Center for American Intercultural Studies where he is helping to develop curricula in intercultural and multicultural education. Prior to joining Iowa State, Dr Adeleke taught at several institutions including Ohio State, Loyola (New Orleans), Tulane, North Carolina State and Montana. He has researched and published extensively in such critical areas as Black Nationalism, Pan-Africanism, Afrocentricity, Black Biography, and African American identity. He is a scholar of global reputation whose publications have provoked critical acclaim and reviews. He has travelled and lectured extensively in Africa, Europe, North America and Australia. He is listed in *Who's Who in American Higher Education* and *Who's Who in the Humanities*. He is also a past President of the Southern Conference on African American Studies.

[2] Esiaba Irobi, "The Problem with Post-Colonial Theory: Re-Theorizing African Performance, Orature and Literature in the Age of Globalization and Diaspora Studies," *Sentinel Literary Quarterly*, vol. 2, number 1, October 2008.

of redemption. Within this genre are the works of classical post-colonial theorists from Frantz Fanon, Edward Said, Aimé Césaire, down to Albert Memmi and Kwame Nkrumah. These scholars helped define the contours of post-colonial theory, revealing the impact of colonialism on identity, culture, and the socio-political conditions of the colonised. More significantly, they mapped out the dynamics of counter-hegemonic discourse critical to engaging and transcending the trappings of the colonial worldview.[3]

Specifically, in relation to Africa, post-colonial theory, *inter alia*, analyses the relationship between Africa and Black Diaspora within the discourse of alienation. Works in this genre examine the roots, sources and strategies of modernity as well as explore the dynamics of the anti-hegemonic ethos. Due to the transnational character of the colonial enterprise, discourse on post-colonial empowerment has often involved strategies of strengthening transnational and transatlantic unity and solidarity.

Post-colonial theorising also constructs modernity as both an ideology and moment of resistance. The quest for, and strategies of, attaining modernity are therefore constituent elements of post-colonial theory. Applied to Africa, it could be argued that post-coloniality and post-modernity exist simultaneously and are mutually reinforcing themes which interrogate Africa-Black Diaspora experiences within the context of mutuality and convergences such as transnationalism and transatlanticism are dominant in post-colonial scholarship on Africa. This is clearly reflected in both the pioneering works of Nkrumah and Nyerere and in more recent scholarship. These works examine the historical and changing contexts of the African/black diasporic intellectual and ideological relationship, as well as the growing complexity and problematic of Africa and its dias-

---

[3] Frantz Fanon, *The Wretched of the Earth*. Paris: F. Maspero, 1961; *Black Skin, White Masks*. New York: Groove Press, 2008 (Revised edition). Kwame Nkrumah, *Consciencism: Philosophy and Ideology of Decolonization*. New York: Monthly Review Press, 1970. Aimé Césaire, *Discourse on Colonialism*. New York: Monthly Review Press, 2001. Edward Said, *Orientalism*. New York: Vintage Books, 1979; *Culture and Imperialism*. London: Chatto, 1993. Albert Memmi, *The Colonizer and the Colonized*. Boston: Beacon Press, 1967; *Decolonization and the Decolonized*. Minneapolis: University of Minnesota Press, 2004.

poric extensions. Nurtured and sustained by shared historical and cultural experiences, this relationship nonetheless manifests complexities and contradictions. It is evident from recent studies that preoccupation with, and the search for, establishing a framework for mutuality in a global context are still perceived as inherently Eurocentric, hegemonic and threatening, and remains the dominant theme in Africa's post-colonial and post-modernist thought.[4] Written within this genre, the essays in this book help illuminate critical forces and moments in the construction of the post-colonial and post-modern theories and ethos in Africa.

In the first essay, "Theorising the Modernist Moment of New African Intellectuals: From *Imvo Zabantsundu* (1880s) to *Drum* Magazine (1950s)," Ntongela Masilela focuses on those he identified as New African Intelligentsia (NAI), and their contributions to the construction of modernity in South Africa. The group includes John Langalibalele Dube, Pixley ka Isaka Seme, Ezekiel Mphahlele, Solomon Plaatje, R. V. Selope Thema, Don G. S. Mtimkulu, Henry Nxumalo, H. I. E. Dhlomo, his brother R. R. R. Dhlomo, Tiyo Soga, Jordan Ngubane, Albert Luthuli, Rev. W.B. Rubusana, H. Selby Msimang, Charlotte Manye Maxeke and Alfred Xuma, among several others. Awareness of the role of modernity in Europe's triumph over Africa undoubtedly motivated their quest for modernity. Collectively they seemed to have concluded that Africa had no choice but to embrace modernity. All of them, according to Masilela, emphasized education, civilisation and Christianity as forces of modernity. In consequence, they all sought education, many going abroad to study before returning to South Africa to apply their knowledge and resources to engaging the problems and challenges of modernity. In other words, emphasis on education inspired the NAI to seek education abroad in order to be better prepared to engage the task of modernity. The education they acquired, therefore, became the foundation for advancing modernity.

---

4   Aubrey W. Bonnett and G. Llewellyn Watson, eds., *Emerging Perspectives on the Black Diaspora*. Lanham: University Press of America, 1990. Ronald Walters, *Pan-Africanism in the African Diaspora: An Analysis of Modern Afrocentric Political Movements*. Detroit: Wayne State University Press, 1997. B. F. Bankie and K. Mchombu, *Pan-Africanism/African Nationalism: Strengthening the Unity of Africa and Its Diaspora*. New Jersey: Red Sea Press, 2002. Kofi Agorsah and G. Tucker Childs, *Africa and the African Diaspora: Cultural Adaptation and Resistance*. Bloomington, Indiana: Authorhouse, 2006.

Masilela identifies four major phases in South Africa's trajectory to modernity. The first phase was the Xhosa Cultural Renaissance, 1870 to 1900, which was spearheaded by Tiyo Soga, who Masilela describes as the first modern African intellectual in South Africa. Next came the New African Renaissance, which lasted from 1905 to 1945, and the Sophiatown Renaissance, 1950 to 1960. The final phase was the Staffrider Literary Generation, 1976 to 1988. The four phases, therefore, constituted the framework for modernity in South Africa. Tiyo Soga was the first South African black to study abroad, at the University of Glasgow. He returned to South Africa infused with modernist consciousness and aspirations. Also, according to Masilela, he was the first to confront the historic tension between modernity and tradition. Instead of jettisoning tradition, Soga opted for a reciprocal relationship with modernity. He considered tradition an indispensable ally of, and springboard for, modernity. His writings emphasised issues that would shape intellectual discussions among future generation of the NAI. Soga concentrated on developing the Xhosa sense of history and nationhood. Others, who also went abroad and returned to become part of the modernist development, included Charlotte Maxeke, who went to Wilberforce University in the 1890s, and John Dube, who studied at Oberlin College.

These members of the NAI were not only inspired by European modernism, but also learned from, and transplanted, the strategies and values of New Negro modernism (i.e., Black Americans). In this respect, Masilela underscores the adjacency of New Negro and NAI modernity. The former heavily influenced the latter. Black Americans, according to Masilela, had attained modernity much quicker. Despite its horrific and dehumanising nature, slavery had rescued Black Americans from the conservatism and retrogression of tradition, and launched them on a quicker path to modernity. In consequence, Black Americans became much more homogeneous and thus were able to achieve modernity at a much quicker pace than Africans who had to contend with the negative and retrogressive consequences of tradition. The successes and accomplishments of the likes of W. E. B. Du Bois and Booker T. Washington became signposts for the NAI. Many of them transplanted into South Africa institutions and strategies derived from the Black American experience. For example,

John Dube's Ohlange Institute, which became the training and nurturing ground for generations of the NAI, was patterned after Washington's Tuskegee Institute. He also published a newspaper, the *Ilanga lase Natal*, which assumed the character of Washington's paper. Generations of the NAI acquired their intellectual voices in the pages of the *Ilanga*. Thus, the examples and accomplishments of Black Americans were instrumental to the NAI's construction of modernity. In other words, South African modernity is inconceivable without New Negro modernity.

The NAI seemed to have borrowed from two sources. First, they imbibed the imperative of modernity and the means from the Europeans. Second, they were inspired by, and invoked, the techniques and strategies of Black American modernity. These educated Africans had the lessons and experiences of Black Americans in focus and as a reference point. John Dube and Pixley Seme both admired Washington's philosophy of education and self-help, industrial achievement and respectability—ideals that they transplanted to South Africa. After his studies, John Dube returned home to establish the Ohlange Institute. Alfred B. Xuma studied at Tuskegee Institute in Alabama, and later wrote his autobiography, *The Story of My Education*, which was fundamentally a tribute to Washington's *Up from Slavery*.

Although acquiring and disseminating education was critical, the NAI also used newspapers as media of developing and sustaining modernist values and consciousness. Many of the NAI were journalists—Allan K. Soja, Walter Rubusana, Solomon Plaatje, Selope Thema, etc. Newspapers such as the *Ilanga lase Natal*, *Umteteli wa Bantu*, *Drum*, *Inkundla ya Bantu*, *The Bantu World* and the *Tsala ea Batho* became important training grounds for the NAI, as well as organs of protest, and of educating, organising and socialising the masses. They were also fundamental to forging intellectual linkages and constructing unifying nationalist consciousness in response to European modernist forms of oppression. Furthermore, newspapers also served as outlets for critical political essays and commentaries, and as a means of inspiring South Africans through exposure to the accomplishments of Black Americans. The careers and achievements of distinguished Black Americans such as Du Bois, Washington, George Washington Carver, Langston Hughes, James Weldon

Johnson, Louis Armstrong, and Charles Drew were given wide publicity in South African newspapers in order to encourage and inspire Africans. Thus, through the pages of the newspapers, these members of the NAI endeavoured to uplift fellow Africans from the depth of ignorance and oppression and instill a self-deterministic disposition for full citizenship. Masilela identifies Selope Thema as the key ideologue of the "New African" perspective in the making of modernity in South Africa. Along with H. I. E. Dhlomo, Solomon Plaatje, and H. Selby Msimang, Selope Thema took part in theorising on the pages of the *Umteteli wa Bantu* about modernity in South Africa.

The members of the NAI sharply disagreed on what role, if any, tradition (i.e., chiefs) should play in the construction of modernity. Some, like Tiyo Soga, Pixley Seme, John Dube and Solomon Plaatje, assigned a prominent role to chiefs as instruments and agents of modernity. Others, however, such as Albert Nzula, H. I. E. Dhlomo and Selope Thema, denounced chiefs as the antithesis of modernity. A few others, however, essentialised a fundamentally different challenge. Charlotte Maxeke, for example, described the principal task of modernity as the liberation of African women from the stranglehold of tradition.

Arts and entertainment also featured prominently in South Africa's drive for modernity. Paradoxically, the members of the NAI were divided on this issue. For example, Emily Motsioleo of the Sophiatown Renaissance demonstrated a deep respect for arts and entertainment in the construction of South African modernity. Curiously, according to Masilela, earlier generations of the NAI did not quite appreciate the importance of these media, especially jazz. The Dhlomo brothers, Selope Thema and Solomon Plaatje, for example, were disdainful of jazz and seemed more inclined toward European classical music. It was not until the 1950s that the Dhlomo brothers began to embrace and appreciate jazz. This leaning toward European art and entertainment reflected the enduring and profound effect of the broader context within which these members of the NAI were educated and socialised. It also underscored their validation of European models and strategies of modernity.

Pixley Seme studied at Columbia University, where he launched the "New African Renaissance" with the publication of his "The Regeneration of Africa." The concept "regeneration" had been popularized in the mid-19th century by New Negro intellectuals such as Martin Delany and Alexander Crummell. This borrowing from, and invocation of, the ideas of New Negro intellectuals became a critical feature of modernist theorising among the NAI. The concept "New African Renaissance" was itself inspired by the New Negro "Harlem Renaissance." Also, the concept "New African" derived from the American "New Negro." In the 1940s, the *Ilanga lase Natal* under Dhlomo developed the idea of the New African Talented Tenth, borrowed from Du Bois' Talented Tenth doctrine. Selope Thema titled his autobiography *Up from Barbarism* as a tribute to Washington's *Up from Slavery*. There was also Peter Abraham's modelling of *Mine Boy* after Richard Wright's *Native Son*. Furthermore, the Sophiatown Renaissance, the culminating phase in the making of South African modernity, and as Masilela contends, a historical experience all earlier phases had been preoccupied with achieving, was undoubtedly an attempt to replicate the cultural texture and achievement of the New Negro Harlem Renaissance. Masilela's essay clearly underlines the cross fertilisation of ideas between the NAI and New Negro intellectuals—the existence of a kind of transatlantic ideological and intellectual lineage, with the NAI invoking the experiences and resources of New World Negroes. In a sense, the construction of modernity in South Africa reflected very much the path taken by New Negro modernism.

In the second essay, "African Intellectuals and the Development of African Political Thought in the Twentieth Century," Mbukeni Mnguni analyses the historical moment of intellectual resistance to colonialism and imperialism which resulted in the development of ideologies and theories of resistance—Pan-Africanism, African Socialism and Nationalism. The pattern of African political thought reflected the transnational character of the colonial/imperial world against which it was directed. According to Mnguni, African political thought sought to transcend national boundaries toward transnationalism. In other words, transnational and transatlantic ideologies and theories of resistance seemed to dominate. Several of the intellectuals whose ideas and writings helped shape the contours of

African political thought in the 20th century included W. E. B. Du Bois, Frantz Fanon, Albert Memmi, Aimé Césaire, Eduardo Mondlane, Kwame Nkrumah, Leopold Senghor, Marcus Garvey, Steve Biko, C. L. R. James, Julius Nyerere, Nelson Mandela, Albert Luthuli and Oliver Tambo. They represented diverse intellectual and political traditions—Pan-Africanism, African Nationalism, Black Consciousness, African Socialism, African Marxism and Negritude. Mnguni identifies Pan-Africanism as the most important. Applying Gramscian analysis, he contends that during the struggle against classic colonialism and imperialism, most African intellectuals were of the organic model which identified with the oppressed. In the post-colonial and neo-colonial contexts, however, there emerged a tradition and model intimately tied in interests and aspirations with the oppressor class.

Fanon contextualised the evolution of African intellectuals within African political history. He identified three phases in their evolution to historical calling: *assimilation, questioning and rebelling,* and *national identification or national liberation.* During the first phase, according to Mnguni, African intellectuals allied closely with the colonial and imperial interests. Mnguni identifies Blaise Diagne of Senegal as a prototype of this tradition. In the second phase, however, African political thought became critical of colonial ideas and assumptions. Leopold Senghor and the ideology of Negritude—a literary movement with profound cultural and political implications—exemplified this critical genre and tradition. As Mnguni suggests, the intellectuals of this second phase forged a historical bond with the people, a bond that would facilitate the eventual defeat of colonialism and imperialism. In his view, this phase witnessed the development and maturation of critical African political thought. It is clear, therefore, from Mnguni's analysis that the first phase of African political history did not produce a critical intellectual tradition.

It was, however, with the emergence of Negritude in the second phase that something similar to a counter-hegemonic intellectual ideology rooted in Africa emerged. Negritude reflected a bonding with Africa. This bond became the precursor for the third and final stage in the evolution of African political thought—that of the national liberation struggles. This phase consisted of a mixed group of political theorists—intellectuals, thinkers and leaders who identified with the political practice of the masses. Colonialism was the main catalyst and focus. This group included Fanon, Cabral, Nyerere, Sékou Touré, Mondlane etc. Fanon and Cabral were the most notable. Both men theorised on the dynamics of revolution. Fanon identified the peasantry, instead of the working class, as the revolutionary class. Cabral, on the other hand, identified the peasantry as the leading physical force, but the working class as the leading historical force. Fanon's major contribution, according to Mnguni, was his critique of the role of the national bourgeoisie. Cabral's major contribution was the distinction between culture and history, and emphasis on culture as the essential element of a people's history. Despite their differences, both Fanon and Cabral converged toward Marxism, an ideology that became central to post-colonial discourse.

Mnguni exalts Pan-Africanism as the most important and critical of the ideologies. Pan-Africanism sought to develop strong cultural, historical and political linkages between Africa and the Diaspora. Though of diasporic origin, Pan-Africanism was soon transplanted to the African context after the Manchester Congress of 1945, due largely to the efforts of Du Bois and Nkrumah, with renewed emphasis on African unity and global black liberation. With the independence of Ghana, Nkrumah assumed leadership of Pan-Africanism, firmly emphasising its transnational imperative. Paradoxically, Pan-Africanism soon collapsed, due in part to its inability to deal with the practical and psychological problems inherited from colonialism. Africans could not develop the sense of collective identity necessary to override ethnicity. In other words, Pan-Africanism failed, Mnguni argues, because it could not deal with the problems and challenges of post-colonial underdevelopment.

Mnguni's essay illuminates two distinct categories of political theory. The first includes those that predated the independence of many African countries. Theories such as Pan-Africanism and Negritude were largely forged and propelled by the contradictions of the imperial-colonial relationship. The second category is African socialism, which emerged due to internal contradictions in many independent countries. Though there are several variants of this theory, Mnguni focuses on Nyerere's, which was formulated in opposition to historical materialism, which he felt did not address African problems. Post-colonial contradictions compelled many African political theorists to revise their ideas. Nkrumah for example shifted from Pan-Africanism to historical materialism and, in the process, his perspectives began to converge with those of Fanon and Cabral. Clearly, Mnguni underlines a certain dynamic with respect to African political thought in the 20th century: its complexity and adaptability to changing historical contexts and circumstances.

Like Masilela's essay on the NAI, South Africa also provided for Mnguni a context for analysing the development of critical political consciousness and ideology. Two individuals dominated this context: Steve Biko, student leader and founder of Black Consciousness, and Nelson Mandela, African National Congress (ANC) leader. Biko was a confluence of Fanon, Cabral and other political movements of the 60s. He and Mandela both theorised about the challenges of freedom and democracy in South Africa. Though their immediate focus was South Africa, they envisioned a continental and global application and ramification of their vision. Mandela theorised on political freedom, Biko on cultural consciousness. Though their perspectives differed, their goals were essentially similar: freedom first in South Africa and, by extension, the rest of Africa. According to Mnguni, both men represented the culmination of the political and cultural process pioneered by Dube, Luthuli and others. In other words, the modernist epistemology that Masilela analysed was indeed a continuum that resurfaced in the Black Consciousness ideology of Biko and other activists of the 60s. On the intellectual level, the struggle in South Africa was a continuation of the contribution to the development of African political thought and modernity whose ultimate goal was the political and cultural unity of Africa. These thinkers are all tied together by existential challenges and struggles, and their ideas and theories were aimed at illuminating strategies for overcoming those challenges. Like Masilela's, Mnguni's essay interrogates the role of intellectuals in the pursuit of modernity. As applied here, the concept modernity denotes rescue or release from the vestiges and stranglehold of colonialism and imperialism, as well as negotiating the tension between tradition and modernity. The works of Fanon, Nyerere, Memmi and Nkrumah, in different ways, deal with these challenges—the 20th century theorising of counter-hegemonic consciousness and ideologies of liberation. Since European hegemony was predicated on theories and ideologies that transcended national boundaries, several 20th century African intellectuals tended to gravitate toward Pan-Africanism or other forms of unifying, counter-hegemonic ideologies.

In the final contribution "African Languages: Obstacles to Internationalism or Additional Wealth for the World?" Jubulani S. Maphalala discusses the prospect for continental and black diasporic unity built upon a foundation of shared and unifying languages. While Masilela and Mnguni concentrate on the modernist aspirations and themes in the political thoughts of African intellectuals, nationalists and post-colonial theorists, Maphalala decides instead to focus on one element that he deems crucial to continental and black diasporic unity: the adoption of a common language. He laments the decline and marginalisation of African languages. Despite Africa's preeminence in civilization, her languages are on the verge of extinction. He is especially critical and resentful of the continued dominance of colonial and imperial languages even in the post-colonial context. The constitutions and political culture of Africa are still framed by colonial languages, languages that were, and remain, vehicles of control and foreign hegemony. He cites the example of South Africa where, despite independence, African languages are still marginalised while the languages of the white ruling class remain dominant. Maphalala argues for the building of stronger continental and diasporic unity upon a foundation of shared languages. He attributes the decline and imminent extinction of African languages to colonial machinations and post-colonial neglect. He advocates the restoration and preservation of African languages as progressive elements that would serve to unify and strengthen Africa and Diaspora blacks. The thrust of his argument is that African languages could in fact serve as globalising and unifying elements for Africa and blacks in Diaspora.

In Maphalala's view, therefore, the quest for continental and diasporic unity would remain elusive without a common language rooted in indigenous culture. He believes that the foundation for projecting this linguistic force globally already existed. Despite centuries of transplantation and separation, blacks in America, Brazil and the Caribbean still retain elements of African languages. Unfortunately, Maphalala laments, these blacks continue to communicate, socialise and be educated in the oppressive and culturally destructive languages of the dominant, white society. Focusing on the theme of unifying ethos, Maphalala describes African languages as inherently unifying, and thus emblematic of the cultural essence of Africa. Unfortunately, these languages are threatened with extinction by deliberate acts and neglect. Maphalala advocates reversing this trend and restoring African languages to prominence and preeminence as vehicles for constructing and solidifying both continental and black diasporic unity.

Unity, genuine independence, and meaningful freedom would remain elusive to Africans and blacks in Diaspora, Maphalala contends, due to historical and contemporary indoctrination and the continued socialisation in the languages and cultures of the oppressive ruling class. Africans and Diaspora blacks have imbibed self-destructive Eurocentric values, resulting in crippling psychological and philosophical dependence on Europeans. Continued education in the languages of the ruling class would further disconnect Africans from indigenous roots and deepen the crisis of what Maphalala characterizes as destructive "cultural AIDS," that is, the wholesale adoption of negative, foreign, cultural ideas and behaviours with the consequent destruction of African culture and extinction of indigenous languages, inducing a total dependence on foreign languages and cultures. Under this condition, Africans and Diaspora blacks would also remain disadvantaged economically since commerce, industry and government are conducted in the dominant imperial languages.

Maphalala urges Africans to stand up and not allow their languages and cultural identities to be destroyed by globalisation and multilingualism. Developing a common language would enable Africans to better resist the force of globalisation and combat the equally destructive force of "cultural AIDS." He advocates an aggressive policy of strengthening African languages as means of education, commerce, governance and communication. This would set the foundation for developing a strong sense of collective identity not only within Africa, but also in the Diaspora. He recommends the identification of four popularly spoken languages that would become continental languages to replace the colonial ones.

All three essays engage not only the ideological underpinnings of Africa's modernism but also the forces and factors involved. In this respect, they are grounded in the works of such classic, post-colonial theorists like Frantz Fanon, Aimé Césaire, Albert Memmi and Edward Said, whose writings provided the framework for understanding Africa's modernist thought and helped shape the contours of post-colonial discourse in Africa. In their expositions on the character of colonialism and imperialism, and analysis of the modalities for overcoming them, Fanon, Césaire, Nkrumah, Nyerere and Memmi establish the guidelines and framework for critical counter-hegemonic discourse.

Their writings provided the NAI in South Africa, and generations of African nationalists and activists elsewhere, the ideological foundation for counter-hegemonic theorising and analyses on the critical imperative for transnational and transatlantic unity. Since Africa was the geopolitical contextual frame for colonial enterprise, *ipso facto*, it became a fertile ground for post-colonial and post-modernist theorising. All three essays underscore the mutually reinforcing and symbiotic nature of post-colonial and post-modernist theorising in Africa. In other words, they establish the post-colonial as the foundation and context for modernist and post-modernist discourses.

With respect to Africa, post-modern theory has focused intensely on themes of transnational unity and identity, and identifying strategies for overcoming challenges of regionalism, ethnicity, religious intolerance, and other divisive, primordial forces. Developing a strong continental and diasporic relationship became the foundation upon which Africa and Diaspora blacks sought to solidify a post-modern, counter-hegemonic relationship. Historiographically and thematically, therefore, the essays in this study expand the interrogation of the themes of transnationalism and transatlanticism within the African and Black Diaspora world. They not only examine the roots and traditions of post-colonial theorising, and the attendant quest for modernity, but also illuminate the underlying factors in Africa's post-modern discourses. It is clear that even in the post-modern era, the overarching goal remains the quest for a Pan-African, Africa-Black diasporic world.

Collectively, these essays demonstrate how African intellectuals have invoked their resources to strategise about modernity in post-colonial Africa. They were all inspired by a consciousness of mutuality that transcended geographical space and historical time. Shared experiences and challenges led to common pools of ideas and patterns of modernist discourse. Most critically, as the essays establish, it is difficult to understand Africa's move to modernity without understanding the Black American experience. This study is unique in that it is perhaps the first to clearly establish, and argue for, this linkage between African modernist protest thought and that of Black Americans. They illuminate how the protest tradition of blacks in America became viable for Africans. Furthermore, they underscore a fundamental paradox of modernist discourse in Africa: the aversion to, and rejection of, European values and hegemonic ethos while being culturally rooted in, and invoking, those same European ideals. All three essays are also rooted in broader post-colonial discourse.

Acknowledgments

Although I did not suggest the topic, the authors of the articles in this book all focus on the pioneering work of African scholars on African politics and each article illuminates the historical development of African political thought in the twentieth century. Ntongela Masilela's "Theorising the Modernist Moment of New African Intellectuals: From *Imvo Zabantsundu* (1880s) to *Drum* Magazine (1950s)" details the most significant contributions made by African intellectuals in newspapers and magazines. Mbukeni Herbert Mnguni's "African Intellectuals and the Development of African Political Thought in the Twentieth Century" investigates the interrelatedness of African political parties and their struggles against colonialism. Jabulani S. Maphalala's "African Languages: Obstacles to Internationalism or Additional Wealth for the World?" examines the problems faced by African languages as they compete against former colonial languages. All of these essays discuss the backgrounds, purposes and interrelatedness of the African intellectuals who formulated our political thought in the twentieth century. I trust that the articles included in this book will stimulate our new thinking about the development of African politics in the twentieth century.

As the editor of this collection of essays, I would like to express my gratitude to the following people: Dr Nozipho E. Makhathini, Mr Noah P. Khathi (M.A.), Prof. Hanns-Lüdecke Rodewald, Sipho and Stefanie Fuhr for their helpful comments. I also wish to express my gratitude to Professor Dr Christoph Wulf, who helped me revise the essays that make up this book.

Mbukeni Herbert Mnguni   September 2015

Part One

Theorising the Modernist Moment of New African Intellectuals: From *Imvo Zabantsundu* (1880s) to *Drum* Magazine (1950s)

Ntongela Masilela[1]

> *Rather than as an isolated activity within the range of social activities, the function of journalism should be conceived as a collection of all functions that, materially or morally, interest the social organism. ... There has never been an institution in the world so entirely identified with society's complex development as, in our era, the institution of the journalistic Press.*
> Jose Enrique Rodo, "How a Newspaper Should Be," *El Telegrafo*, September 24, 1914.

> *I have always studied the style and thought of this wonderful journal. (I call it wonderful because it is an unsurpassed effort of a single-headed Native, edited and supported by Natives and thus proving Native capacity and genius when given a chance.) During my study I got very much interested in the writings of one 'Amicus Homini Gentis' who as late as 1930 gave us his well selected notes that gave much variation among the writings of men like Rev. Dr. A. H. Ngidi who wrote very scientifically.*
> B. Wallet Vilakazi, "What Writers Has This National Paper?" *Ilanga lase Natal*, March 17, 1933.

> *On his return to South Africa, he was appointed sub-editor of the once famous Abantu-Batho, an African journal which played a very important part in our politics during the twenties of this century and it is from his association with this journal that his career of serious journalism starts. ... His best writings which have come down to us are drawn from the first ten years of Herzog's rule, when*

---

[1] Ntongela Masilela, Ph.D., is Professor of English and World Literature and Professor of Creative Arts at Pitzer College in Claremont, California, USA and Adjunct Professor of African American Studies at the University of California in Irvine, USA. He has taught at the University of Lodz in Poland, and at the University of Nairobi in Kenya. He is the co-editor of *To Change Reels: Film and Film Culture in South Africa*, Wayne University Press, 2003. He is editor of the book *Black Modernity*, Africa World Press.

> *African intellectuals took a leading part in discussing the problems of their people.*
> *In the host of intellectuals who influenced our thinking in those times, Mr. Thema was the only one who was as practical as he was realistic in his approach.*
> Jordan K. Ngubane, "Richard Victor Selope Thema," *Inkundla ya Bantu*, July, Second Fortnight, 1946.

This construction of the possible mapping of the African intellectual structure as a system in South Africa would not have been possible without the efforts of the recent modern masters, H. I. E. Dhlomo (in the 1940s), Z. K. Matthews (in the 1960s), Jordan K. Ngubane (in the 1980s), and Ezekiel Mphahlele (in the 1980s), each of whom possessed great intellectual authority. Their intellectual portraits are of recent vintage. There are earlier intellectual portraits. There is one by Pixley ka Isaka Seme on Walter Rubusana written a year before he launched the ANC (*Imvo Zabantsundu*, January 24, 1911). Another, on Richard W. Msimang, originally appeared in *Abantu-Batho*, and although anonymously written, it appears to have been written by someone with a deep knowledge of the British legal system, and this could only have been Pixley ka Seme (the other British trained attorney Alfred Mangena hardly wrote any intellectual essays); it was reprinted in Solomon T. Plaatje's *Tsala ea Batho*, July 15, 1913.

In the portrait of Walter Rubusana, Pixley Seme emphasises the classical education he received at Lovedale, winning first and second prizes in Latin, Greek, Hebrew, Logic, Church History and Philosophy ("Biographical Sketch: Rev. W. B. Rubusana, Ph. D., M. P. C."). He notes also the doctorate degree received through correspondence for the 'research document'—not really a 'book'—*History of South Africa from the Native Standpoint* (a text completely lost, not obtainable in the United States or in South Africa) from the McKinley University based in Chicago. After a three-year search for the document and the University here in the United States, this author received credible and authoritative documents from the Illinois Office of Higher Education that this was a bogus 'University' located in a ghetto house. What precipitated the closure of this 'Institution' was a letter written from South Africa by a white American in the 1950s complaining that Dr Jacob Nhlapo (naturally his dissertation *Intelligence*

Tests and the Educability of the South African Bantu is also untraceable) had obtained a doctorate from McKinley University in the 1940s and demanding from the Illinois Office a confirmation of its legitimacy. After a long procrastinated battle of about 15 years, McKinley University closed its doors in 1966. It had been open since the late 19th century.

The black University was closed ostensibly for unfair economic practices. The American had obtained his degree from McKinley Roosevelt University, a white institution also based in Chicago. A note of historical interest: Having obtained his first degree from McKinley Roosevelt University and a doctorate degree from Syracuse University, Eduardo Mondlane, founder of FREELIMO and father of the Mozambique nation, tragically assassinated by Portuguese colonialists in 1969, wrote to the president of his alma mater denouncing that quite a few Africans in South Africa were obtaining bogus degrees from McKinley University, thereby lessening the value of those obtained from 'real' universities.

In emphasising the kind of education Rubusana had had, Seme was showing the quality of education (formal or self-taught) necessary for a successful negotiation of the historical experience of modernity. Concerning his work as an ordained minister, Seme marvels at his translation into Xhosa of ecclesiastical documents, as well as his contributions to literary journals of London Societies. The whole tradition of translating Western religious and allegorical texts and documents into Xhosa had been initiated by Tiyo Soga, as will become evident below. Lastly, Seme salutes Rubusana for participating in politics, especially for having been elected the first President of the Native Congress of South African in 1909. Very astonishingly, Pixley ka Isaka Seme wrote the following words, which were high praise indeed coming from him:

> [A]nd today the citizens of Tembuland unite in honouring his past record and service by raising him to sit in one of the most important Councils in the great Union of South Africa. Indeed a happy sign to this fatherland, and one which should calm many a troubled breast, proving as it does that white men can and will recognize ability even in a black man. This is indeed a rich signal for hope to those who work and pray for the *regeneration of Africa*, which alone can give us a great South Africa that is the Africa in which the white man and black man, though different, shall both work, respect, and help one another.

(my italics) (Pixley Isaka ka Seme, *The Regeneration of Africa*. April 5, 1906, Colombia University)

Pixley ka Isaka Seme was alluding to his landmark essay of 1905, "The Regeneration of Africa," which in effect launched the New African Movement in South Africa, as argued fully elsewhere, and partly below. In hailing Walter Rubusana as a regenerator of Africa, Pixley ka Isaka Seme was designating him as a New African.

Perhaps the inspiration for the intellectual portrait of Richard William Msimang by Pixley ka Isaka Seme was the former's compilation of a booklet on behalf of the newly established ANC (then a political organisation of only a year old and known as the South African Native National Congress) showing the catastrophic effects of the *Natives Land Act of 1913* on Africans. Msimang explains the necessity of the document in the following manner:

> The immediate purpose and object of compiling together few instances … for they are comparatively very few instances of actual cases of hardships under the Natives Land Act 1913 is to vindicate the Leader of South African Native National Congress from the gross imputation by the Native Affairs Department, that they make general allegation of hardships without producing any specific cases that can bear examination. In other words, the charge is, they make wild statements of existing hardships which they fail to support by concrete facts. ("Explanation Notes," *Natives Land Act 1913: Specific Cases of Evictions and Hardships*, etc., Authority of the Records Committee of the South African Native National Congress, [no date; mostly probably 1914 or 1915]; reprinted by Friends of South African Library, Cape Town, 1996)

Msimang's legal training in England enabled him to write a superb document. One of the most important facts that emerges from Seme's portrait is that Richard Msimang was one of the first two boys with whom John Dube opened Ohlange Institute in 1901 ("The New Solicitor: Mr. R. W. Msimang"). Msimang's subsequent career and achievements: mastering English Jurisprudence, becoming the first African from South Africa to qualify as a Solicitor of the Supreme Court of Judicature in England, being an Attorney in the Transvaal Province, opening his private firm of attorneys, as well as taking over as legal advisor to the Native National

Perhaps this long influence should not be totally surprising given the terms of an anonymous obituary in *Ilanga lase Natal*:

> Death has removed from us a great scholar, educationist and a wise man. We have suffered irreparable loss in his death at a time when an outstanding leader of his type is so greatly needed to bring about desirable relations between the black and white races of this country. ("Death of Dr. Aggrey," September 9, 1927).

Without a shadow of a doubt, he was instrumental in shaping the political imagination of New African intellectuals, though many would argue in a very conservative direction. As just one instance of the extraordinary impact he had on New African intellectuals, in a long threnody in 1947 in memory of the recently departed Benedict Wallet Vilakazi, exactly twenty years after James Emman Kwegyir Aggrey's own death, H. I. E. Dhlomo invoked his name in the galaxy of great African intellects and heroes:

> Black bards and heroes greet their friend and peer; / Great Shaka, Magolwana there appear; / Mbuyazi, Aggrey, Dube, Mqhayi, ache; / To meet him … so Bambatha, his name sake; / Not these alone, for here below he loved; / And spoke with long-haired bards, among them moved; / Now Keats, his idol, whom he prayed to meet; / Chaste Shelley, too, come forth our Bard to greet; / And Catholic great Dante, Comedy; / Divine enjoying, smiles to meet and see; / A Catholic bard mate ("Ichabod: Benedict Wallet Bambatha Vilakazi," *Ilanga lase Natal*, November 8, 1947).

By the time H. I. E. Dhlomo wrote his innumerable portraits in *Ilanga lase Natal* in the 1940s, the tradition of constructing intellectual portraits as a way of formulating a discourse on history by New African intellectuals had been in existence for nearly half a century. His major contribution to this generic form was to embellish some of the portraits with a deep psychological profile of the concerned figure. In this new configuration of the form, Dhlomo had a great rival in his close friend Jordan K. Ngubane (cf. *The Modernity of H. I. E. Dhlomo: South Africa in the Modern World*, forthcoming, Oxford University Press, where I attempt to compare their brilliant styles in the construction of all the intellectual portraits they ever wrote). Dhlomo's intellectual portraits of Benedict Wallet Vilakazi, John Dube and Albert Luthuli are on the same conceptual level as Ngubane's of

Anton Lembede, Albert Luthuli and A. W. G. Champion. They differ in a marked way from the 'old-fashioned' style of R. V. Selope Thema's famous sketch of Pixley ka Isaka Seme, and Solomon T. Plaatje's numerous portraits of chiefs, who were in their own way 'intellectuals.'

We should add that Jordan Ngubane not only wrote portraits of Africans; in *The McGraw-Hill Encyclopaedia of World Biography in 12 Volumes* (1973), he has contributions on the Union's first Prime Minister Louis Botha (vol. 2, pp. 98–100), on another former Prime Minister James Barry Muntz Herzog (vol. 5, pp. 244–45), on yet another Prime Minister Daniel Francois Malan (vol. 7, pp. 111–12), and also on Chief Lobengula of the Ndebeles (vol. 6, pp. 542–43), and on King Moshweshwe of the Basotho nation (vol. 7, pp. 541–43).

Likewise, Dhlomo also wrote portraits of Europeans. Perhaps the best way of tracing the deep affinities between Ngubane and Dhlomo is by looking at the way they wrote about the New African journalists whom they thought to have been exemplary in the way they carried out their tasks. In his brilliant intellectual portrait of Jordan Ngubane, A. P. Mda analysed the complex relationship between Anton Lembede, Jordan Ngubane, himself, and Benedict Wallet Vilakazi, but inexplicably does not mention H. I. E. Dhlomo. This essay is startling in its self-assured certainty and dazzling foresight:

> Once he came out openly in support of African Nationalism, the triumph of that outlook was assured, and it is common knowledge that the emergence of African Nationalism altered the complexion of politics in South Africa. ("Jordan Ngubane," *Drum*, May 1954)

Jordan Ngubane, as the editor of *Inkundla ya Bantu* in the 1940s, invited H. I. E. Dhlomo to join him in writing three portraits of famous journalists they had known. Ngubane chose R. V. Selope Thema, who was in the 1930s and 1940s editor of *Bantu World*, John Dube, who had founded *Ilanga lase Natal* in 1903 and had been its editor for decades, and Ngazana Luthuli, who succeeded Dube in 1917 and was himself replaced on his retirement by H. I. E. Dhlomo and R. R. R. Dhlomo in 1943. Tragically, only one of H. I. E. Dhlomo's contributions survived, that on his brother to whom he was assistant editor at *Ilanga lase Natal*. This author believes one of the other contributions was on Solomon T. Plaatje, editor of *Koranta ea Becoana*, *Tsala ea Becoana*, *Tsala ea Batho*, about whom H. I. E. Dhlomo, elsewhere, wrote this short but astonishing obituary (arguably the best intellectual portrait he ever penned, or, for that matter, the best by any New African intellectual on another New African intellectual):

> A great, intelligent leader; a forceful public speaker, sharp witted, quick of thought, critical; a leading *Bantu* writer, versatile, rich, and prolific; a man who by force of character and sharpness of intellect rose to the front rank of leadership notwithstanding the fact that he never entered a secondary school; a real artist, passionate, as sedulous, alert, keenly sensitive … Such were the qualities of the late Mr. Sol. T. Plaatje whose death will be deeply mourned in literary, social, political, and religious circles throughout British South Africa. I shall ever remember my last talk and ramble with him. For several hours we discussed as we talked from one place to another, fulfilling his sundry engagements … so well known was he, so highly esteemed, so dearly beloved.

Again:

> He spoke of his many literary plans. Now he is no more, and there is nobody to fill his place. Never have I found him autocratic, contumacious, or narrow of outlook. Whatever subject he touched upon … leadership, literature, travel, amusement … was treated with a brilliancy, humour, ability and finish that at once surprised and captivated, inspired and humbled me. Of his many achievements and understandings I leave it to better and more experienced pens to tell. ("An Appreciation," *Umteteli wa Bantu*, June 25, 1932)

Dhlomo was to write another intellectual portrait with such intensity and passion exactly two decades later in 1952 in *Drum* magazine in remembrance of Benedict Wallet Bambatha Vilakazi, as though saying to the Sophiatown Renaissance writers and intellectuals in writing in their intellectual forum, here is a real intellectual who could be a bridge between yourselves and our generation of New African Renaissance artists and thinkers (of course, the notions or categories of Sophiatown Renaissance and New African Renaissance are designations and reconstructions of much later decades).

Dhlomo wrote several portraits of Vilakazi, in the form of a review, an appreciation, an obituary and a critique, either in a poetic form or in prose ("Nature and Variety of Tribal Drama," *Bantu Studies*, vol. XIII 1939; "Benedict Wallet B. Vilakazi, M. A.," *Ilanga lase Natal*, January 15, 1944; "Dr. B. W. Vilakazi: Poet," *Ilanga lase Natal*, March 30, 1946; "Snaps: Dr. B. W. Vilakazi," *Ilanga lase Natal*, August 16, 1947; "Dr. B. W. Vilakazi," *Ilanga lase Natal*, November 1, 1947; and "Ichabod" as already mentioned).

Dhlomo constructs his major portrait of Vilakazi in *Drum* by outlining the obsessive way his great friend and interlocutor desperately wanted to acquire Christianity, Western civilisation, and education, the very constructs which nearly a hundred years before Tiyo Soga had theorised as being of vital importance to Africans' acquisition and construction of modernity. In this quest Dhlomo was in fundamental agreement with Vilakazi. This clearly indicates that there was a direct line of continuity stemming from Tiyo Soga running through the Xhosa Cultural Renaissance to the Zulu Intellectual Renaissance and beyond.

Besides the differences among other things, the contrastive emphasis on different generic forms—one on the essay the other on poetry—while the Xhosa Cultural Renaissance was enthralled with the 'English Renaissance' of Milton, Bacon and Shakespeare, the Zulu Intellectual Renaissance was mesmerized by the Romanticism of Shelley and Keats. Besides his love of Keats and Blake, Dhlomo was amazed that Vilakazi added his love of Virgil, whom he learned to read in the original language of Latin. Vilakazi's preoccupation with Latin culture was so profound that he eventually converted from Protestantism to Catholicism (*Drum*, July 1952).

This tremendous drive for academic success of Vilakazi and Dhlomo postulates as partly deriving from the psychological scars of having being rejected by some of his New African peers for not having attended Fort Hare University, which was then considered by the black middle class as the premier University for Africans. To avenge this slight, Vilakazi obtained his first degree from a premier white University, Witwatersrand. He excelled so well in his academic work that he wanted to pursue further doctoral studies in literature at Cambridge University or Oxford University. In this, he was frustrated by the white government and lack of financial support. He obtained a doctorate in literature from the University of Witwatersrand with an extraordinary dissertation, *The Oral and Written Literature in Nguni*, and while still a student, he co-wrote a major *Zulu-English Dictionary*. While pursuing his academic studies, he published three Zulu novels and wrote some of his major poems.

Although Dhlomo implicitly criticises him for not fully engaging himself with African politics as he should have, he sought to dispel the notion that Vilakazi was a 'Right Wing scholar.' Benedict Vilakazi wanted to build a consensus among New Africans through an example that would put education and academic scholarship in the first tier of achievements of African modernity:

> His first reactions to city life in Johannesburg must have been those of a shocked and disillusioned man. He found a sophisticated African Society little interested in academic degrees as such, but in talent and achievement in all walks of life. A talented jazz band leader or successful business man were ranked higher than an unproductive graduate and were more popular and respected. (H. I. E. Dhlomo, "An Appreciation", *Umteteli wa Bantu*. June 25, 1932)

Benedict Vilakazi set out to be the greatest scholar of African literature(s) and cultures, and succeeded in achieving this. Dhlomo was fascinated by Vilakazi's genius in all its facets. Although Dhlomo does not note this, Vilakazi mentions in one of his essays that it was in reading African newspapers that he found his precursors who inspired him in his intellectual endeavours:

> It is very interesting to study the trend of thought espoused by Native papers and sometimes to discover how editors hold together the minds of the writers of their papers. ... I have always studied the style and thought of this wonderful journal. (I call it wonderful because it is an unsurpassed effort of a single-headed Native, edited and supported by Natives and thus proving Native capacity and genius when given a chance.) During my study I got very much interested in the writings of one 'Amicus Homini Gentis' who as late as 1930 gave us his well selected notes that gave much variation among the writings of men like Rev. Dr. A. H. Ngidi who wrote very scientifically ...

> Then comes MR. R. R. R. Dhlomo who has long patronised the paper and whose writings unto this day still hold good. One thing I like with this writer

is that he is reading a novel with an open eye to everything that happens round him. He is good in political reports and criticisms. There is one thing he has not done for the *Ilanga lase Natal* ... his short stories have so far not been there published.

And:

Now I can say the *Ilanga lase Natal* is dominated by the opinions of Mr. Josiah Mapumulo. Several times have made mention of the name of this gentleman in this and other journals. We, who are writers for the *Ilanga* should copy this from this gentleman: To read and pore on books, and absorb knowledge from newspapers both old and new and never to say that we are grown old and tired of reading and reproducing. Many a time have I envied his quotations and wished I would turn a burglar to search his library of old books of history of many mission stations, both Protestant and Catholic. There is that lucidity in his writing which is un-sailed with bias and un-cramped by party opinions. His work should be continuous he must pioneer for the journal which is a living symbol of a black man's ability. ... We are now engaged in an age wherein we begin to want to know the why and wherefore of everything ... let us observe for ourselves and examine all facts and find their laws, and try to express them in our own ways to meet the demands of our concepts within this changing Africa. ("What Writers Has This National Paper?," *Ilanga lase Natal*, March 17, 1933)

It needs to be added that H. I. E. Dhlomo has not as yet been taken seriously as a brilliant literary critic, as he undoubtedly was, but his specifying the influence of A. H. Ngidi on Benedict Vilakazi, and their incorporation of European classic tradition (Greek and Latin poetic traditions, both read in the original language) into Zulu modern poetry, shows him to have possessed an acute critical imagination ("Dr. Ngidi," *Ilanga lase Natal*, August 18, 1951).

With these formulations, an appreciation of an emergent, modernist, intellectual heritage, Benedict Wallet Bambatha Vilakazi was clearly aware that the New Age of Modernity demanded new intellectual and cultural practices which he himself was to exemplify in the subsequent fifteen years. His actual exemplification of the intellectual demands of modernity was to have profound impact on two major intellectuals: his contemporary, A. C. Jordan, the incomparable novelist and scholar, arguably the one New African intellectual who was conscious in the twentieth century of the legacies of the Xhosa Cultural Renaissance of the nineteenth century; and Mazisi Kunene, a major force in the subsequent generation, whom it would not be an extravagant claim to characterise as the greatest African poetic voice in the twentieth century.

Dhlomo's preoccupation with historically locating Vilakazi in the intellectual tradition that in the modern times began with Magema M. Fuze and intersected with those founded by Tiyo Soga and Solomon T. Plaatje was part of his situating himself and Vilakazi in the New African tradition. Dhlomo's serious engagement with historical location through the greatness of Vilakazi was evident to other New African intellectuals, as can be seen in the intellectual portraits of Dhlomo and Vilakazi in poetic form by Walter M. B. Nhlapo.

What was so extraordinary about H. I. E. Dhlomo's understanding of the complex structure and contours of Vilakazi's creative imagination was his awareness of it being preoccupied with similar issues as those that informed Tiyo Soga's historical and cultural project of the middle of the nineteenth century:

> After what interval of Time is a nation in the state of barbarism in what the Kaffir's are after the introduction of Xty [Christianity] & civilization, to begin to ascend the scale of human progress and enlightenment ... When should a nation, begin to improve in civilization after its introduction? Had the Europeans never set their feet in Kaffirland & allowed only the missionaries to introduce the gospel ... wonders would have been wrought ... & no *doom* of the Kaffir race would be pronounced ... There is a destructive civilization ... that civilization which when it comes into contact with Barbarians ... seeking to profit by their ignorance, what in fact ... seeks its own good ... not their good ... this civilization must come into collision with the natives ... of course the natives must fair worse ...
>
> It has been thus in Kaffirland ... The gospel has been interfered with ... its good has been neutralized ... the vices of Civilization, have been introduced ... & never better ... & hence this ... *doom* of the Kaffir ... but the fault of it lies at some other door ... Give me the gospel to any people ... give me Xn [Christian] & civilization *alone* to any people that civilization carried by Christian men ... carried on philanthropically for the good of native ... & the world

would be subdued ... it might take time but it would ultimately conquer ... & it would be unattended by those evils of the civilization I complain of ... ("The Kaffir Race," *The Journal and Selected Writings of The Reverend Tiyo Soga*, (ed.) Donovan Williams, A. A. Balkema, Cape Town, 1983, p. 39-40)

Vilakazi was to forge the dialectical unity of tradition and modernity in such a unique way that its achievements have as yet to be exhausted. Paradoxically, Benedict Vilakazi's criticism of H. I. E. Dhlomo's conceptualisation of African literary modernity underlines the pertinence for our time of his achievements ("African Drama and Poetry," *The South African Outlook*, July 1, 1939, pp. 166-7).

H. I. E. Dhlomo's intellectual portrait of John Dube presented a different set of historical problems related to modernity. Writing an appreciation under the pseudonym of "X" about a year and a half before John Dube's death, inspired by the essay "Negro Americans: What now?" in which James Weldon Johnson, though acknowledging the great achievements attained by African Americans despite enormous adversities, still felt they were not exercising their fullest capabilities and not utilising their talents to the utmost, Dhlomo felt that the situation was similar in the instance of Africans in South Africa. Dhlomo was not so much arguing that the attainments of these two African peoples were comparable, since he had no illusions about the greater achievements of African Americans, but rather that their full potential had not been fully maximised in their differently adversarial conditions. Implicit here was that Africans should learn from African Americans.

Dhlomo examines the literary and historical works of Dube as an instance of a New African intellectual using the utmost power of his imagination to alleviate the suffering of the African people in South Africa. Dhlomo could easily have adduced the examples of Solomon T. Plaatje or S. E. K. Mqhayi or Thomas Mofolo, however much he may have disagreed with their particular ideological perspectives, which was not the case with the first two. Dhlomo praises John Dube for his biography of Shembe and his novel *Insila ka Shaka* for reconstructing South African history from the perspective of Africans. He evaluates the novel as invigorating the Zulu language through displaying its rhythmic musicality, beauty and power

("Dr. J. L. Dube, Ph.D., M. R. C., as Author," *Ilanga lase Natal*, August 19, 1944). He concludes his reflections by indicating that it is the legacy of appreciation of language (both English and Zulu) that John Dube has imparted in *Ilanga lase Natal*.

Having taken the editorship of the newspaper with his brother, R. R. R. Dhlomo, from Dube's successor the previous year, Dhlomo was very much aware of the high level of seriousness he had to display. Without a shadow of a doubt, his brilliant literary, historical and political essays in the newspaper in the following decade by far surpassed what had been achieved by Dube and his success or from anyone in the previous forty years. In other words, he exhorted his fellow New African intellectuals a goal he himself set out to realise. That H. I. E. Dhlomo is acknowledged today as one of Africa's greatest intellectuals in the twentieth century can only be an indication of how seriously he set out to utilize to the maximum his intellectual potential.

Having founded Ohlange Institute in 1901, at which outstanding young New African intellectuals such as Rueben Caluza and Richard Msimang, among others, were educated before going overseas for further education, and having also founded *Ilanga lase Natal* in 1903, thereby making it possible three decades later for the Young Lions of the New African Movement such as Benedict Vilakazi, Jordan K. Ngubane and R. R. R. Dhlomo to find their intellectual voice (H. I. E. Dhlomo on his part really found his voice on the pages of *Umteteli wa Bantu* under the 'tutelage' of R. V. Selope Thema and H. Selby Msimang), it is not surprising that the death of John Langalibalele Dube in February 1946 was felt by the majority of these two succeeding generations of intellectuals as marking the closing of a particular phase in the historical understanding of modernity.

Whereas the other figures of the intellectual generation of John Dube, such as Walter Rubusana or Solomon T. Plaatje, still largely clamoured to posit the adjacency of modernity and tradition—not one predominating over the other—as evident in their continuing belief in the paramount importance of African Chiefs within the imperatives of modernity, those of the generation of H. I. E. Dhlomo, Anton Lembede and A. P. Mda were unyielding in their conviction of the irrelevancy of chieftaincy in the modern era. Despite this fundamental, generational difference, Benedict Vilakazi, Jordan K. Ngubane, Martin Kumalo, K. E. Masinga and L. L. Kumalo wrote within a matter of weeks of John Dube's death a commemorative booklet of essays, poems and songs paying homage to him.

In one of his many short notes paying respect to the passing of Dube, H. I. E. Dhlomo commends this younger generation of New African intellectuals for wanting to continue with the political and intellectual tradition which John Dube had initiated ("Young Men On Dr. Dube," *Ilanga lase Natal*, March 2, 1946). What was so extraordinary about John Langalibalele Dube was not only that he subscribed to the edict of Tiyo Soga's that African modernity can only be realised through education, civilisation and Christianity, and inspired by African Americans, he actually constructed institutional forms (a newspaper and an academic institution) which concretised for many Africans the lived experience of modernity. Dhlomo has written two major appraisals of John Dube, an essay and a brilliant analytical poem. The long poem includes the following lines:

> Great son of streams and valleys African!
> Mafukuzela! thou of warrior frame;
> Whose rare achievements proved
> the Black Man can!
> You thought and thought and
> wrought us into fame.
>
> Of battles fierce great scholar,
> author, sage
> Find time the muses fair to serve.
> Our mist
> Of ignorance you raised, Light of our age!
>
> Pray, poets of our Race play softly on
> Your harps! Lay down your shields
> for he is gone!
> Pipe dulcet songs of praise to God upon
> Your tender strings as Fuze passes on
> To join immortal throngs of those who strove
> With tears to serve both God and Man;

He now belongs to the immortal few
Who on the Tree of Time their names did hew
With blades of beauty, pain and noble deeds;
In service to their people and their needs;
Such Shaka, Aggrey, Khama, Hannibal
Where Fuze won by deeds, some climb by tricks.

He battled with clean arms of sanity,
Where now we suffer shafts of crudity;
The Ego and the shout are all to-day;
The Nation thirsts—
while pygmies prance and play!

("John Langalibalele Dube: Two Songs," *Ilanga lase Natal*, February 23, 1946)

Although Dhlomo places John Dube in the illustrious company of heroic figures such as Shaka, Hannibal, for him the actual intellectual progenitor of Dube was Magema M. Fuze. In the second line to the Prologue of his book, *Abantu Abamnyama Lapa Bavela Ngakona (The Black People and Whence They Came)*, the first important work written by an African in the Zulu language, Fuze commends John Dube for having founded *Ilanga lase Natal* and thereby bringing within a coherent historical perspective the national aspirations of the African people.

Given that the book, popularly known as *Abantu Abamnyama (The Black People)*, was written a few years after the turn of the twentieth century, although first published in 1922, Fuze had deep foresight in seeing Dube's institutional creation as gathering and consolidating the kind of information and knowledge that would enable the African people to have a better understanding of the modern era which was in the process of dawning (trans. H. C. Lugg, edited by A. T. Cope, University of Natal Press and Killie Campbell African Library, Durban, 1979, p. i). In other words, Fuze was well conscious of the important role of newspapers in consolidating the historical perspectives and cultural aspirations of the African people. Isaac Bud-M'Belle in the Cape noted in his booklet, *Kafir Scholar's Companion* (1903).

Abantu Abamnyama was an attempt to forge a synthesis of the history of the Zulu Nation. In the Epilogue, written in 1922, the only part of the book written at this late date, when he was over eighty years old and very doubtful whether he would ever see its publication, he wrote the following:

> Concerning my own deliberations, gentlemen, I now suggest that we immediately prepare for the benefit of our future generations a record of events to show them where they came from. A grasshopper when it is fertilized at the end of a year and when it feels that it is about to die, digs a hole in the ground and lays its eggs there and covers them with soil, and then settles on a twig to wither and die. After a time the eggs hatch out, and its children emerge as grasshoppers just like it. We should remember that on death we do not come to an end, but by our progeny we renew ourselves to continue indefinitely, and so arise anew as if we were beginning at the beginning. (p. 147–8)

The historical novels of R. R. R. Dhlomo are a continuation of a historical sensibility initiated by Magema Fuze, a historical sensibility articulating the complexities of transition from tradition to modernity. Possessing a thoroughly modernist sensibility, H. I. E. Dhlomo could only seriously identify with Fuze as representing the disappearance of his intellectual origins. H. I. E. Dhlomo's historical sensibility was more in tune with Thomas Carlyle and W. E. B. Du Bois than with that of his compatriot. His reference to Fuze in some of his reflections on Zulu language and literature had more to do with his calibrating the texture of Zulu artistic sensibility from Fuze through A. H. Ngidi to Benedict Vilakazi than with his own sense of historical location. In this vein, it is interesting what Vilakazi has to say of Fuze in his magisterial dissertation of 1946, *The Oral and Written Literature in Nguni*:

> Though the title is wide in its import, the whole book is an ethnographic history of Nguni tribes, ... and it omits the other Bantu peoples ... Though most of Fuze's material is what may be found in many English and Afrikaans books of an earlier date, there is an original contribution in which Fuze looks critically at certain matters and offers an explanation of his own. The book too contains much valuable poetry, but it is badly recorded, as verse form is not observed. (submitted to the University of Witwatersrand, p. 294–5)

The fundamental criticism Vilakazi makes of Fuze is that he was governed by the imperatives of tradition rather than of modernity. Consequently, his historical vision was still wedded to Zulu nationalism rather than articulating the perspective and ideology of African Nationalism. Its poetic sensibility leaves much to be desired; this is the reason Benedict Vilakazi compares it unfavourably to Walter Rubasana's *Zemk'inkomo Magwalandini* (1911). The one issue on which Vilakazi was in agreement with Fuze was that the launching of *Ilanga lase Natal* by John Dube had revolutionised African political and cultural consciousness by forging an ideology of 'United African Action,' which was concretised by the formation of the ANC in 1912 (then the South African Native National Congress), and the newspaper had given an expressive forum to such writers and intellectuals such as A. H. Ngidi, Theodore Myeza, R. R. R. Dhlomo and others (p. 280–1).

Given this monumental role of John Dube with *Ilanga lase Natal* in the cultural and political imagination of the African intelligentsia, which was preoccupied with the construction of modernity in South Africa, it is not surprising that H. I. E. Dhlomo's final tribute to him is one of the finest, if not the greatest, tribute by one New African intellectual about another New African intellectual ever to appear in any kind of newspaper. Undoubtedly, this tribute constitutes arguably the greatest prose piece ever written by H. I. E. Dhlomo ("Dr. J. L. Dube, Ph.D., M. R. C.: A Tribute," *Ilanga lase Natal*, February 23, 1946). This tribute perhaps ought to be the model of African intellectual portraits. This tribute gave Dhlomo an occasion to postulate his theory on history, derived from Du Bois' concept of the Talented Tenth and Thomas Carlyle's notion of Hero worshipping, that it is individuals who determine the course of history, not the masses or collectives.

For him, John Dube was a classic exemplification within an African context. Dube himself in wishing to be judged by absolute standards, as Dhlomo indicates, had an implicit acceptance of the Du Boisian construct. Dhlomo makes it clear that Dube expected and wanted to be judged on the basis of the following criteria: "Do not judge me by the heights I have attained, but by the depths from which I have come." This Booker T. Washingtonian principle not only indicates the enormous debt the African owed to the American, as we have alluded to above, but also the very fact that New Africans intervened in the construction of South African modernity on the basis of historical principles initially formulated by the New Negroes.

Dhlomo praises Dube for having discovered his philosophy, uniqueness and strength through overcoming the 'disabilities' and 'ideologies' of tradition societies: superstition, regimentation, uniformity and conservatism. Dhlomo characterises this building of bridges from tradition to modernity by Dube as "a great epic poem, a symphony" that defined his freshness, originality and consistency. It is in this bridge building that Dhlomo sees Dube as having inspired Rueben Caluza and S. E. K. Mqhayi. In lifting the veil of backwardness from his people, Dhlomo argues that Dube faced a much greater task than Washington, because whereas African Americans were more homogeneous, Africans had always been heterogeneous.

These considerations lead Dhlomo to observe that despite the savagery of slavery, it had at least 'freed' the African Americans from the conservatism and regressiveness of custom. For Dhlomo, these two factors accounted, among others, for the historical differential of why African Americans achieved progress into modernity at a much quicker pace than Africans. Dube had greater obstacles and difficulties than Washington in uplifting the masses. Despite the historical differences in the circumstances they encountered, Dube was a great student and disciple of Washington. Dhlomo wrote with great admiration for Dube's consistency in facilitating for African people to attain progress. He enumerates the upheavals and crises Dube had to encounter again and again, and from each encounter he emerged stronger and wiser. To Dhlomo this was what characterised the nature of great men in history. Dhlomo concludes by observing that in being a true democrat and statesman, Dube was no longer merely a prominent leader, but had become for Africans a national symbol and institution. In believing that Africans and Europeans could live peacefully together, Dhlomo indicates that Dube stood for a united South Africa.

In constructing this extraordinary portrait of John Langalibalele Dube within the purview of the historical achievements and influences of Booker T. Washington, Dhlomo was drawing attention to the necessary adjacency of New Negro modernity and New African modernity. Although Dhlomo was more conceptually articulate in constructing the connections, many other New African intellectuals postulated other forms of linkages. In *The Oral and Written literature in Nguni*, Benedict Vilakazi argued that the ideology of literary form exemplified in the writings of Langston Hughes had many lessons for the forging of a 'national spirit' by New African writers:

> These writers, with the exception of H. I. E. Dhlomo in his poetry, fail to universalize their particular political handicaps and to transform them into a generalized suffering, expressed symbolically in poetic or prose forms. In prose it should be easy to follow the example of Langston Hughes, who, though dealing with a Negro colour bar, race-discrimination and lynching, yet writes without bitterness or vituperation, and with such simplicity and restraint that few readers of any race are able to put down his books unmoved. To English readers, Hughes' short stories especially are a revelation of the injustices of which even decent white people are capable and of the horrible sadism of the oppressors. ("What Writers has this National Paper?" *The Oral and Written Literature in Nguni*. A dissertation. University of Witwatersrand. 1946)

In the work of Langston Hughes we have the dominant note of the new Negro spirit in writing, where the topics are treated generally without allowing didactic emphasis or propagandist motives to choke their sense of artistry. While there is much to be learnt from Negro artists by our African writers in English, we may nevertheless praise them for what they have achieved, for most of them have gained their knowledge of journalism from mere reading (Pixley Isaka ka Seme, *ibid.*, p. 283–5).

Arguably, no New African intellectual felt the impact of New Negro modernity greater than Alfred B. Xuma, who spent three years, 1913–16, studying at Tuskegee Institute, which enabled him subsequently to study medicine at white, elite American universities. As his biographer demonstrates remarkably well, the influence of New Negroes on the last President-General (1940–9) of the ANC before the ideology of the Youth League enveloped the national organisation was deep and profound, ranging from Xuma's autobiographical essay, "The Story of My Education," which was modelled on Booker T. Washington's *Up From Slavery*, to his major address, "Some Lessons from America," to the African elite at the Bantu Men's Social Centre in 1933, an audience which in all certainty included H. I. E. Dhlomo:

> Though their numbers were small, the educated African elite exerted a disproportionate share of influence on black politics in Johannesburg. They assumed that their education and 'modern' outlook qualified them to speak on behalf of their race. Part of their political commitment sprung from the fact that, like all Africans in South Africa, they also faced difficult housing conditions, pass laws, discrimination, and racism. The lessons of black America loomed large in the minds of these educated Africans. John Dube and Pixley Seme had long admired Booker T. Washington, whose gradualist vision of racial progress stressed education and self-help. ... From black America, Xuma drew upon the notions of self-help, education, respectability, and individual achievement to tailor a message of race progress for black South Africans. Few of his compatriots had absorbed Booker T. Washington's Tuskegeean work ethic as enthusiastically as had Xuma. But unlike Washington, Xuma was not an accommodationist, and did not believe his fellow blacks should remain content with a separate and unequal citizenship. (Steven D. Gish, Stanford University dissertation [1994], *Alfred B. Xuma, 1893–1962: African, American, South African*, p. 101, p. 115)

Given that these were some of the ideological and historical principles that characterised New Africanism, it is not surprising that H. I. E. Dhlomo wholeheartedly subscribed to them.

In fact, in one of his intellectual portraits of Albert Luthuli, in the form of an Open Letter, H. I. E. Dhlomo wanted to know what he was doing to facilitate an exchange and intellectual discourse between the New African intellectuals and the New Negro intelligentsia at the moment of their constructing their respective modernities:

> For it is true that we must depend for our success on the few who have done so much, have much to do, to do more. The many who have so much time on their hands that they can do much, will never have time to do anything. Life is measured, not by time, but by achievement. ... You are [a] chief. Frankly, what is your opinion about the maintenance of tribalism in a modern democratic and acquisitive society? What is the line of demarcation between a tribal or rural African and the urban African worker? These are crucial subjects for they concern policy and the future of the African race. ... On your return from the U. S. A., one of the points was that little was known there about

Africa. What do you propose should be done about this? How can our writers help? Is it not possible to get fellowships for some of our talented men to go abroad and remedy this? ("Weekly Letter: To Chief A. J. Lutuli," Busy-Bee [H. I. E. Dhlomo], *Ilanga lase Natal*, April 1, 1950)

This letter was written at a very critical moment in the history of the African people in their struggle for liberty, equality and freedom: at the moment when Albert Luthuli was replacing A. W. G. Champion as President-General of the provincial African National Congress in Natal, and Dr James Moroka was replacing Dr Xuma as the President-General of the national organisation of the ANC, for the latter did agree with the implementation of the Programme of Action of 1949 as proposed by the Youth League. This Open Letter was part of a secret campaign by Dhlomo to turn Luthuli against Champion. As revealed in the *Unpublished Autobiography of Jordan K. Ngubane* (in the Carter-Karis Collection; mispaginated and some pages missing), both he and Dhlomo, in their respective newspapers *Inkundla ya Bantu* and *Ilanga lase Natal*, undertook a secret campaign to destroy the reputation of Champion who, through incompetence, authoritarianism and corruption, was destroying the provincial organisation. The several intellectual portraits of Albert Luthuli written by H. I. E. Dhlomo were not only undertaken with this political aim in mind, but were an expression of his admiration for him as an exemplary figure of the New African Talented Tenth.

Writing on the occasion of the dismissal of Albert Luthuli as a Chief by Henrik Verwoed, then a Minister of Native Affairs, because he had refused to terminate his membership of the ANC and had also declined to renounce his election to the General-Presidentship of the organisation, Dhlomo, writing under the pseudonym of "Busy-Bee," paid tribute to him as a profoundly principled person. Not wishing to repeat what he had earlier written on him, he wrote tongue-in-cheek: "Only recently my journalistic colleague, H. I. E. Dhlomo wrote about Chief Luthuli and race relations. I shall not repeat what this writer said, save to say this ..." ("Albert John Luthuli," Busy-Bee, *Ilanga lase Natal*, November 15, 1952).

Saying something new, Dhlomo enumerated a distinguished roll of his achievements: President of the Natal Teachers' Union, head of the Zulu

Cultural Society, President of the Natal Bantu Farmers' Association, President of the Native Reserves Association, and leading member of the South African Christian Council. These attainments revealed to Dhlomo that Luthuli was a paragon of a New Leader, a leader capable of grappling with the complexities of modernity which the African people were facing.

It was with anger and dismay that Dhlomo wrote of Henrik Verwoed's refusal to meet with Luthuli, the Minister giving voice to the viewpoint that on assumption of the leadership of the ANC Luthuli had shifted from being a 'moderate' leader to being an 'extremist' one. Writing with indignation, Dhlomo remarked: "In other words, Luthuli must betray the trust of the whole African Race and go hat in hand begging for forgiveness for having been sane and bold enough to seek human and democratic rights for his people in the country of their birth" ("Verwoed and Luthuli," Busy-Bee, *Ilanga lase Natal*, August 1, 1953). What Dhlomo profoundly appreciated in Luthuli was the moral seriousness of his leadership qualities as a New African Leader.

The last political and intellectual portrait of Albert Luthuli by H. I. E. Dhlomo had originally been commissioned by R. V. Selope Thema for the newspaper he edited, *The Bantu World*, which was published in Johannesburg, but the popular demand was such that R. R. R. Dhlomo had to reprint it in Durban's *Ilanga lase Natal*. In this sketch, Dhlomo characterises him as belonging to an African School of Thought that believes in honest cooperation and principled compromise, and as a profound realist and, consequently, an interpreter and solid bridge between Africans and Europeans. It was this ideological outlook which made him a wise, progressive and reliable leader. For Dhlomo the greatness of Luthuli lay in overcoming the severe obstacles imposed by the white government in the process of African people creating and constructing modernity, as well as succeeding in many ways to resolve the contradictions that were perpetually threatening the unity of the African people in their attempt to overthrow oppression. In gratitude to him Dhlomo wrote:

> Luthuli grew in stature and usefulness ... There was malleability, height and progressive ripeness in this growth. First, he proved a wise progressive and reliable administrator in a field where often he found himself between the

Scylla of his people's conservatism and scepticism, and the Charybdis of official impatience and superiority ... complex cynicism ... Then came the plunge into the grim, boiling vortex of Congress or racial politics. First there was the exhausting experience of serving under Mr. Champion at a time when great changes and a clash between the old and the new were the order of the day. To an ex-educationist accustomed to discipline, rationality and principles: a devout Christian averse to any but clean ways and methods; and a mediator-interpreter believing in the middle course, all this must have weighed 'heavy as frost and deep almost as life' on Luthuli. (H. I. E. Dhlomo, "Portrait of Today: Chief A. J. Luthuli," *Ilanga lase Natal*, September 6, 1952)

With these words Dhlomo confirms what Jordan K. Ngubane was to write a decade later in his *Unpublished Autobiography*, that both of them seeing Luthuli as representing the future vision of African Nationalism, aligned with modernity hence progressive and rational, they made certain in their respective newspapers' columns that he would prevail within the ranks of the ANC. This document contains an extraordinary portrait of Luthuli by Ngubane, written immediately after the devastating defeat of African Nationalism by Afrikaner Nationalism at the great battle symbolised by the Sharpeville Massacre of 1960.

The success of H. I. E. Dhlomo and Jordan K. Ngubane in participating in the defeat of A. W. G. Champion and the triumph of Albert Luthuli, as well as assuring the hegemony triumph of African Nationalism over Marxism (Communism) within the ranks of the New African Talented Tenth of the ANC, merely confirmed their belief in the central role of the African newspapers in shaping the modern consciousness of the African people. One could add in parenthesis that Dhlomo's hostility toward what he considered a corrupt and decrepit form of Champion's African Nationalism never abated in later years; if anything, it intensified, because he felt it undermined the African Nationalism he supported, that of the ANC Youth League ("Mr. Champion's Blatancy And Bankruptcy," by Busy-Bee [H. I. E. Dhlomo], *Ilanga lase Natal*, January 8, 1955). Champion responded with equally virulent hostility ("Busy-Bee Groaning with Political Aims," *Ilanga lase Natal*, January 22, 1955).

One could contrast Dhlomo's lambasting of Champion's intellectual dishonesty with his warm portrait of Z. K. Matthews in the context of editorialising the Professor's realism, integrity and persistence in portraying the terrible living conditions and circumstances of Africans.

Tracing the genealogy of R. R. R. Dhlomo's intellectual development, Dhlomo begins by placing him in the tradition of New African intellectuals who were both journalists and men of letters, as exemplified by Allan Kirkland Soga, Walter Rubusana, Solomon T. Plaatje, R. V. Selope Thema, Jordan K. Ngubane and others. One distinguishing feature of R. R. R. Dhlomo separating from this eminent group is that he never considered himself an intellectual, scholar or philosopher, despite having written outstanding Zulu historical novels on Shaka, Dingane and Mpande. H. I. E. Dhlomo believes that this self-evaluation on the part of R. R. R. Dhlomo, who never attended political meetings, going instead to concerts or watching films, and preferring to attend cricket games and football matches was wrong. Dhlomo finds this paradoxical because he states that his brother was a voracious reader, reading a novel per day, and had a passion for writing.

Dhlomo speculates that this self-devaluation by "Rolfes" was perhaps due to his indifference to intellectual discussions and formalities. The other thing which distinguishes R. R. R. Dhlomo from these other members of the Talented Tenth was that although some of them may have contributed articles to white newspaper, "Rolfes" became a correspondent for Stephen Black's weekly, *The Sjambok*, which carried his satires, short stories and articles. Although also having worked for *Ilanga lase Natal* when the newspaper was under the editorship of Ngazana Lutuli in his earlier days, it was only when he worked as assistant editor to R. V. Selope Thema in the 1930s for *The Bantu World* that R. R. R. Dhlomo found his journalistic métier. So much so indeed that Dhlomo states that Benedict Vilakazi considered "Rolfes" the best humourist of the day on the basis of his satirical contributions to the newspaper.

A perusal of R. R. R. Dhlomo's contributions to *Bantu World* clearly show that he was satirising the conflicts and paradoxes between tradition and modernity. By the time "Rollie Reggie" was writing his satires under the name of "Rolling Stone" in the 1940s in a newspaper he edited together with his brother H. I. E. Dhlomo, *Ilanga lase Natal*, their biting and critical edge had fallen off. Dhlomo found the relationship between Selope Thema, truly a great journalist in his early days as a columnist for *Umteteli wa Bantu* in the 1920s, and R. R. R. Dhlomo fascinating because while the former was violently hostile to tradition and totally enamoured with modernity, "The Pessimist," in spite of his immersion in urban culture, constantly, unrelentingly and valiantly attempted to retain a deep sense of rural tradition.

Selope Thema left an indelible impact on "The Randite." H. I. E. Dhlomo himself, who was to become a great journalist in his *Ilanga lase Natal* days, was mesmerised by R. V. Selope Thema when both were contributors to *Umteteli wa Bantu*. Dhlomo's close friend, Jordan K. Ngubane, who was to become a great journalist for *Inkundla ya Bantu* in the 1940s, found it impossible to escape the towering influence of Selope Thema when he was his assistant editor for *The Bantu World* in the late 1930s, notwithstanding that by that time the Old Man was only a shadow of his former self.

Contextualising and extrapolating on H. I. E. Dhlomo's reflections on the historical moment in which his brother was a representative figure, three observations can be made. Firstly, there is a great tradition of brilliant journalism in South Africa stretching from John Tengo Jabavu's *Imvo Zabantsundu* through F. Z. S. Peregrino's *South African Spectator* and Solomon T. Plaatje's *Tsala ea Becoana* to Ngubane's *Inkundla ya Bantu* and Henry Nxumalo in *Drum* magazine in the 1950s (it is convenient to stop here at the termination of modernity as signalled by the Sharpeville Massacre of 1960) and it is imperative that these writings be assembled in an anthology. Secondly, newspapers have been the most important training grounds of the most formidable African intellectuals, not necessarily universities or academies (one need only think of H. I. E. Dhlomo or Solomon T. Plaatje or R. V. Selope Thema or Jordan K. Ngubane). The most original and creative writing by New African intellectuals was realised in semi-forgotten newspapers, and not books or extant anthologies. The real intellectual history of South Africa is predominantly traceable through newspapers. And lastly, and not least, the profoundest patterns and the deepest structures of the encounter between tradition and modernity were spectacularly captured in the African newspapers.

It is nearly impossible to overestimate the importance which H. I. E. Dhlomo attributed to African newspapers in bringing the African people into the modern age. This is testified to by his production of prodigious essays, be they philosophical, political, cultural or social, in *Ilanga lase Natal* from 1943 to 1955, a year before his death. His writing of the great prose poems, nearly all printed in the newspaper in 1947 (an astonishingly creative year), was an attempt to shape the modernising imagination of the New African Masses with the ideology of modernistic consciousness derived from the poetics of the Romantics, the Symbolists and the Modernists.

Dhlomo was profoundly conscious of the ethical and social responsibility of newspapers in the era of his moment, as evident in several reflections and meditations on the role of newspapers. In the earliest of these, he compared the power of the African newspapers to that of the Church in reflecting the opinions of African people. Given that there was no democratic representation of the African people in Parliament, he believed the newspapers would act on their behalf in expressing their democratic aspirations. Given also that the ANC in the 1940s had no official newspaper organ, Dhlomo sought as much as possible for *Ilanga lase Natal* to express and articulate the views of the national organization. While Dhlomo was striving to achieve this, Alfred B. Xuma, who was President-General of the ANC in the 1940s, saw as one of his major tasks the founding of a national newspaper to be the organ of the organization, since the demise of its own newspaper, *Abantu-Batho*, in the late 1930s.

Although Xuma did not succeed in his endeavour, he sought at one time to buy the controlling interest of *Inkundla ya Bantu*, impressed as he was by the way Jordan K. Ngubane had transformed it into the ideological forum of the ANC Youth League (Steven D. Gish, *Alfred B. Xuma, 1893–1962: African, American, South African*, p. 173–4). One can only surmise that Xuma attached the same paramount importance to newspapers as Dhlomo. Writing on its historic importance in charting the development of the historical consciousness of the African people, Dhlomo noted:

> [The African Press] shapes and directs the thoughts of tens of thousands. It is a better watchdog of African interests than political and social bodies. It is

more alert, articulate, militant and informed ... It does not only spread knowledge, guide and build the Race. It also entertains ... as those who read its regular features of humour in the vernacular know. It forms a unique record of political, sport and other organisations; of the careers and achievements of prominent men and women; of the history, development and trends of Bantu political, social and cultural thought and progress. Here it plays a very important role by filling in the gaps caused by the absence of records of our public organisations, the diaries, correspondence and biographical material of our great and public figures ... In these and other ways the African Press caters for young and old. Christian and non-Christian, rural and urban, literate and illiterate. And for the same reason it is the best gauge and mirror of what the African race as a whole thinks, does and wants. ("Influence And Power Of African Press," *Ilanga lase Natal*, March 3, 1943).

He paid tribute to the leading editors, sub-editors, columnists and freelance journalists who he thought had established and continued this noble and high tradition of the African newspapers. Dhlomo called for the history of African newspapers to be written.

A decade later, on the 50th Anniversary of the founding of *Ilanga lase Natal*, Dhlomo reflected again on the historical responsibilities of the African Press. Unfortunately portions of this later, much longer piece, which was a variation on the Editorial of 1943, and continued in succeeding weeks, have been lost. Written in the context of the Defiance Campaign of 1952, a seminal event in South African history which had a deep effect on him, and alluding to the influence of the New Negroes on New Africans in matters of cultural creation and production, Dhlomo emphasised those aspects of the history of African newspapers that embodied and articulated the protestations of the African people against European racial and economic oppression:

> It should be noted by those who like to make comparisons between the Negroes and the Africans that unlike the United States of America (or any other country for that matter, except the late Nazi and Fascist regimes in Europe), the Constitution of South Africa stands for injustice, discrimination and inequality. This is important. Whatever we may say about the prevalence of discrimination and Jim Crowism in America, the essential and fundamental difference between that country and ours, is that the forces of right and justice, Christianity and democracy, there have the power and authority of the Con-

stitution behind them, whereas here the whole power and philosophy of the Constitution stand against liberty, justice and democracy.

> Such, in brief, is the background of the social and political set-up of South Africa. Thus it was that the leading African newspapers were conceived and born as organs of protest ... to educate, organise, and consolidate the African masses; to educate white Public Opinion; to voice to the world the sufferings and tribulations of the Africans in the land of their birth. ("The African Press," *Ilanga lase Natal*, June 20, 1953)

Taking the cue from him, Dhlomo's magnificent cultural and political essays of the 1940s and 1950s should be included within the South African canon of Protest Literature. In the same year, Dhlomo wrote an Editorial in which he protested the white government's search for pretexts to suppress African newspapers, and chastised some of the European newspapers for aligning themselves with such undemocratic endeavours:

> One of the ironies and contradictions of the South African political situation is that each discriminatory law made against the African rebounds to the detriment of the European. To rob the African of rights and freedoms, the European himself must loose certain rights and freedoms. Things like freedom, justice and democracy ... as every true philosopher from Socrates down to Toynbee has taught ... are indivisible ... Working under great disabilities ... a theme that needs a separate article ... the men behind the African Press are sensitive and jealous about their responsibility. Their reportage is clean, unbiased and correct. Their comment and commentaries, if bold and fearless, are sedate, objective, constructive, restrained, and above all, unchallengeable, based as they are on facts, and not one motion, prejudice and the exploitation of the delicate and explosive South African situation. ("Freedom of the Press," *Ilanga lase Natal*, March 14, 1953)

It was this tradition of objective and engaged African journalism, from Allan Kirkland Soga in *Izwi la Bantu* to Jordan K. Ngubane in *Inkundla ya Bantu*, that H. I. E. Dhlomo saw himself in *Ilanga lase Natal* as affirming and extending.

If with H. I. E. Dhlomo the African newspapers were crucial in facilitating the formation and shaping of modernistic sensibilities among New Africans, principally the traditions of protest and opposition with

Benedict Wallet Vilakazi they were invaluable in forging intellectual lineages. We have already seen how Vilakazi found compelling intellectual tradition delineated and consolidated on the pages of *Ilanga lase Natal* by Rev. Dr A. H. Ngidi, 'Amicus Homini Gentis,' and Josiah Mapumulo. Mapumulo had profoundly impressed on Vilakazi that the construction of an intellectual tradition can only be on the basis of deep, historical knowledge, the cultivation of book culture, the mastery of language and a commitment to an unswerving search for historical truth. Similar to these commitments, Walter M. B. Nhlapo argued that the task of African newspapers should be to pose an intellectual challenge to its readers and act as their guide in the search for truth:

> Newspapers and magazines render the majority of Africans considerable service as reading material, for which Africans should pay tribute and gratitude. But do they represent a true specimen of African ideals, thought, talent and intellectualism? If so, might we not reasonably expect to find in these newspapers and magazines so well patronised with advertisements and so widely read, a spirit which would help to penetrate to the very depth of African thought: music, drama, poetry and politics. If the journals fail to express African thought and achievements, who will? To deny vernacular a place in newspapers would be scarcely in harmony with the body and soul of Africa. The unlettered masses of Africa are the back-bone of the nation ... The newspapers and magazines are a civilizing factor. Civilization can never be really safe without a bodyguard. Not only should a paper be a popular, intelligent or civilized mouthpiece, but be virtuous. The African press as a whole deserves a drastic and general and forthright overhaul if it will serve its cause. ("Language and Matter in the African Press," *Ilanga lase Natal*, November 7, 1953)

Since Walter Nhlapo mentions in passing that his formulation of newspapers and magazines as civilising entities was inspired by a particular article written by H. I. E. Dhlomo, it might be worthwhile to momentarily pause over it. (The October 10, 1953 issue of *Ilanga lase Natal* where H. I. E. Dhlomo's article, "Journals. Language and Matter," appeared has been lost.) In arguing that African newspapers must not only fully participate in the struggle of the African people for freedom and economic empowerment, but must also strive for the elimination of illiteracy among the Africans, Jacob M. Nhlapo was in effect expanding on what Benedict Wallet Bambatha Vilakazi and H. I. E. Dhlomo had formulated, and Walter Nhlapo (no relation) was to formulate as their civilising mission. For Jacob Nhlapo it was *Inkundla ya Bantu* under the editorship of Jordan K. Ngubane which exemplified the better aspects of the civilising process:

> "Khanyisa" [one of Jordan K. Ngubane's nom *de guerre* in this newspaper at this time] statement gives me the courage to say to the *Inkundla ya Bantu* what I have for some time wished to say. I'm sincerely proud of the *Inkundla* because 'it is owned by Africans, edited by Africans, printed by Africans and depends for its growth on African support.' It is my sincere hope and prayer that before long this journal will not only be larger but be published at least twice a week. ("African Press Developments," *Inkundla ya Bantu*, October, Second Fortnight, 1946)

The remarkable achievement of Jordan K. Ngubane in *Inkundla ya Bantu* was his prescience in seeing that the vehicle for civilisation enlightenment had to be African Nationalism as formulated by the ANC Youth League, which was then forging a modern sensibility as well as modernistic political skills for mobilising people on a massive scale. To Jacob M. Nhlapo, as also true of other New African intellectuals, the construction of African Nationalism through the columns and editorials of newspapers was a proper response to the European, modernistic forms of oppression.

In initiating a series of reflections on Famous Journalists in *Inkundla ya Bantu* in 1946, Jordan K. Ngubane was re-initiating a project which had originally been launched by Govan Mbeki, his immediate predecessor in the editorship of the newspaper. Unfortunately, in subsequent years, the project collapsed. In 1941 Mbeki began a series called *Gallery of African Heroes: Past and Present*, which was in effect an examination of the passageways of transformation from tradition into modernity. What Mbeki was doing in *Inkundla ya Bantu* was continuing an intellectual tradition that was perhaps launched by F. Z. S. Peregrino in 1902 in the *South African Spectator* by establishing the portraits of the heroes and heroines in the union of the *Ethiopian Movement* and the African Methodist Episcopal Church. Many African newspapers in the twentieth century seemed to have preoccupied themselves with using biographical sketches to trace the patterns of history.

In the 1920s, *Umteteli wa Bantu* published in its many Supplements innumerable portraits of New Negro writers, intellectuals and artists, including: Mariam Anderson, Roland Hayes, Booker T. Washington, Joe Louis, and W. E. B. Du Bois. In contrast to what the *South African Spectator* had achieved two decades earlier, *Umteteli wa Bantu* published no sketches or portraits of New African church men and women or intellectuals or artists, believing, no doubt blinded by its Americaphilia, that no New Africans approximated the achievements of the New Negroes.

It was left to R. V. Selope Thema in *Bantu World* in the 1930s to rectify the mistakes of the newspaper he worked for as a columnist in the 1920s, by not only publishing the portraits of the achievements of New Negro scientists such as Carver, Just and Charles Drew, but also printing a *Bantu World Picture Gallery* of 'New African intellectuals,' which included, among others: S. E. Krune Mqhayi, Reuben T. Caluza, Griffiths Mitsioloa, Moses Mphahlele, I. Bud-M'Belle, H. Selby Msimang, Albert Nzula, A. W. Champion, D. D. Tengo Jabavu, John L. Dube, and R. R. R. Dhlomo. As though these were not sufficient, Selope Thema now and then published pictures of the ANC Executive Committee, as in the following gallery of 1933: Dr P. ka I. Seme, T. D. Skota, S. M. Makgatho, Z. R. Mahabane, A. Z. Mazingi, T. M. Mapikela, R. V. Selope Thema, C. S. Mabaso, Rev. J. S. Likhing, and H. Selby Msimang.

Continuing with this tradition, *Drum* magazine in the 1950s, the last decade of New Africanism, published an extraordinary series of intellectual, artistic and political portraits, of both New Africans and New Negroes, under the title of Masterpieces in Bronze. This series included: Z. K. Matthews, Kwame Nkrumah, Clements Kadalie, D. D. T. Jabavu, Learie Constantine, Mnandi Azikiwe, Gerard Sekoto, Ethel Waters, Henry Nxumalo, Lionel Hampton, Victor Mkize, John Tengo Jabavu, Louis Armstrong, and Duke Ellington. Taking this tradition to its extreme, *Drum* and its sister newspaper *Golden City Post* serialised the autobiographies of Louis Armstrong and Billie Holiday, respectively, in competition with each other. In 1961 Z. K. Matthews brought this tradition to a close on the pages of *Imvo Zabantsundu* with the survey of the large canvas of the intellectual and political portraits from Elijah Makiwane in the late nineteenth century through Solomon T. Plaatje to Noni Jabavu in the middle of the twentieth century.

With the launching of *Gallery of African Heroes: Past and Present*, Govan Mbeki was revitalizing this tradition of writing history in a biographical form. It was not accidental that he began with Hintsa, the great King of the Xhosa Nation. Mbeki begins the sketch of Hintsa by placing him within the historical context of his time. It was the era of the upheavals of the *Mfecane* turbulence unleashed by Shaka in his quest to unify all of the states and nations in Southern Africa. This was a moment that necessitated visionary leaders like the Zulu King, Hintsa himself, and Moshoeshoe, the King of the Sotho Nation. One major characteristic of this period was the consolidation of African Nations and Kingdoms ("U-Hintsa," *Inkundla ya Bantu*, May 1941).

Besides the *Mfecane* phenomenon, Mbeki emphasises that this happened concurrently with the beginning of the consolidation of British imperial hold in South Africa. Restless under this imperial domination, the Afrikaners were beginning to move northwards on the so-called 'Great Trek' in order, paradoxically, to impose their own form of imperialism on African people. This was truly a historical period of New Beginnings. Govan Mbeki observes that this period had been prophesied by Ntsikana, the '*Great Prophet*,' in the early part of the nineteenth century as the coming times of profound unhappiness. Although Mbeki does not say so in so many words, this was the beginning of the 'Great Divide' between tradition and modernity, of European history imposing itself on African history, or as Amilcar Cabral succinctly expresses it, this was the beginning on the continental scale of Africans being forced to disembark African history and enter European history. It is this 'Great Divide' that is at the centre of the compelling power of Plaatje's Mhudi in which Mzilikazi mournfully laments in his Shakespearean soliloquy that himself belonging in the past and relying on the antiquated knowledge of the medicine men in the face of the overpowering knowledge of modernity cannot cross this continental divide into the future.

Plaatje makes Mzilikazi plead and recognise, against his instinctual feelings and habits of mind, that it is women like Mhudi of the Barolong and Mnandi of the Ndebeles (Matebeles) who will lead the African people into the unavoidable historical moment of modernity. Mhudi anticipates many of the achievements Chinua Achebe was to achieve in *Things Fall*

Apart. Thomas Mofolo, ensconced in the certainties of 'Christian modernity,' in his controversial and powerful novel *Shaka*, makes Shaka's 'blood thirstiness' a direct product of this 'Great Divide,' which he defines in the ideological terms of manicheanism.

Ntsikana was prophesying that what history demanded had to happen. The fascination with Ntsikana of Xhosa intellectuals from Jordan, Govan Mbeki and John Knox Bokwe was because of the invisible divide between history and myth he attempted to articulate. John Knox Bokwe had this to say of Ntsikana:

> All at once, the vision of bright rays which he saw in the morning shining gloriously on the side of his favourite ox, Hulushe, is recalled to his remembrance, and without a single word of intellectuals from A. C. [Hulushe] as explanation, or apology to any one, he orders his people to get ready to return home! All of them, surprised, and whispering puzzled enquiries as to the cause of so early a departure, obey the order and march home, greatly vexed that their pleasure has been so abruptly brought to an end, with no explanation hinted as to the reason why [Ntsikana asked his people to leave a festival in which on three occasions when he tried to participate, a gust of violent wind gathered thereby preventing him from participating in the festivities].
>
> As they neared home, they came to a small river. Here Ntsikana threw aside his blanket, plunged himself into the water and washed off all the red ochre that painted his body. He then proceeded on his way, while his followers were yet more surprised at this additional strangeness and eccentricity of behaviour. That night all the inhabitants of Ntsikana's kraal be took themselves to their huts with not a little to comment upon. This introduced the precedent of washing off the red-clay when any one professes conversion, or of becoming what is sometimes spoken of as a School-Kafir, because he has discarded red ochre for civilized clothing. (Ntsikana: *The Story of an African Convert*, Lovedale Press, Second Edition, 1914, p. 11–12)

The fascination of the two imaginative texts, historical essays in the form of historical narratives, is that they both deal with the 'Great Divide': Ntsikana, with its historical comprehension; and Mhudi, with its historical incomprehension.

Govan Mbeki portrays Hintsa neither as an immediate converter to the new things of the world necessitated by imperial European domination (Plaatje in his novel hints that modernity could have emerged without the precipitating factor of European intervention), nor as an unyielding force wedded to the past, but rather as a historical mediator open to the future yet working to preserve Xhosa "traditions and democratic institutions." One of the things Mbeki finds salutary in Hintsa is that he accepted and embraced the Fingoes, refugees from Shaka's military rule, into the Xhosa nation. Mbeki also notes that Hintsa combined a deep faith in democratic institutions and a profound hatred of British imperial domination in South Africa:

> He was being compelled to disregard his national pride and pave the way for the British troops to annex more land from his people without any loss of life. The choice was now between betrayal of his people and facing death. In order to avoid the stigma of shame that would have long after been associated with his name, he made a dash for freedom and he was shot dead and his body mutilated. Such is the end of those who love freedom, for freedom is God's greatest gift to mankind. He was born in a land of freedom he lived and breathed the free air in a free land. When his freedom and that of his people was threatened there was nothing else left for him but to risk the British bullets and the risk proved fatal, but Hintsa died free that his people might have freedom and have it more abundantly. (Govan Mbeki, "Gallery of African Heroes: Past and Present." *Inkundla ya Bantu*. 1946. H. I. E. Dhlomo, "The African Press." *Ilanga lase Natal*, June 20, 1953)

It is this combativeness against imperialism and the commitment to freedom that Mbeki hoped would be imparted from the 'traditionalism' of Hintsa into the modernity of the African National Congress. There were unfortunately only three subsequent *Gallery of African Heroes: Past and Present* portraits, written by other members of the African intelligentsia, and only one of which approximated the historical depth and intellectual resonance exemplified by Govan Mbeki.

W. M. Tsotsi begins his consideration of Davidson Don Tengo Jabavu by situating his achievements within the Cape intellectuals and political tradition of liberalism. Writing of this tradition, Tsotsi notes:

Prof. Jabavu was born and bred in the old Cape liberal tradition of the Victorian age, when the colour of a man's skin set no limits to his aspirations. This was the heyday of the Native politician, and W. B. Rubusana thought it no shame to sit shoulder to shoulder with Europeans in the Provincial Council. John Tengo Jabavu himself aspired to this position, and it is not to be expected that his son who spent over ten years of his life at the very fountain of this liberal culture would not subscribe to its doctrine of the equality of men. ("Davidson Don Tengo Jabavu," *Inkundla ya Bantu*, June 1941)

For many members of the New African intelligentsia, the Cape liberal tradition came to mishap in 1903 when at the Treaty of Vereeniging concluding the Anglo-Boer War of 1899–1902, the English settlers came to a rapprochement with the defeated erstwhile enemies, the Boer settlers, about the political dangers of the 'black peril,' the very Africans who had been supportive to the English in securing their victory. The other event which in a real sense signalled the end of the Cape tradition as a living philosophy of life rather than as a disembodied ideological system was the Union of South Africa in 1910, which represented in large measure the white South Africans forming a 'New South Africa' at the expense of the political and democratic rights of the African people. Given these blatant betrayals of Africans at the hands of Europeans, Tsotsi argues that this lead directly in later decades to the formation of the ANC (African National Congress) and ICU (Industrial and Commercial Workers' Union of South Africa).

For Tsotsi, these two events spelled a real crisis from which the Cape liberal tradition never fully recovered, despite the tragic sycophancy of John Tengo Jabavu. Within the purview of this dramatic political background, Tsotsi enumerates the achievements of Davidson Don Tengo Jabavu: he set the standard of education for Africans in his time; he represented the African point of view in inter-racial matters; he earned for Africans respect from Europeans; he worked tirelessly in organising Africans; he was the only leader capable of uniting African intellectuals and masses in the All-Africa Convention; he helped to bring to the limelight New African intellectuals such as S. E. K. Mqhayi, the great Xhosa poet; and lastly, he was an inspiration to his students.

Tsotsi also enumerated several books Tengo Jabavu had written: *The Black Problem, Bantu Literature, Life of John Tengo Jabavu, Segregation Fallacy, E-Jerusalem,* and *Native Taxation*. Perhaps because of these attainments Davidson Don Tengo Jabavu seemed to possess an egoism that knew no boundaries or limits. W. M. Tsotsi relates that while travelling on the train with the Professor of Latin and Bantu Studies he suddenly said to him:

> You know, I understand Hitler has a list of the twenty leading Africans whom he intends to destroy the first thing when he comes to this country, and my name is first on the list, man. (W. M. Tsotsi, "Davidson Don Tengo Jabavu", *Inkundla ya Bantu*, June, 1941)

Leaving aside the fantasy of this pronouncement, why would Tengo Jabavu be first on the list, not Clements Kadalie, Pixley ka Isaka Seme, James Thaele, R. V. Selope Thema or John Dube! All this makes one uncertain whether in founding the All-African Convention, Davidson Don Tengo Jabavu was solely motivated by his hostility to the Hertzog Bills or was founding a movement which would rival the ANC, an organization to which his father John Tengo Jabavu and Davidson Don himself had always displayed a studied indifference. All in all, Davidson Don Tengo Jabavu was a pioneer in some of the things he preoccupied himself with concerning New Africanism.

In writing this intellectual portrait, W. M. Tsotsi has written one of the best ever written on New African intellectuals. The other two *Gallery of African Heroes* portraits do not attain the impressive achievements realised by W. M. Tsotsi and Govan Mbeki ("Life of James J. Mateza," Harry Mjamba, *Inkundla ya Bantu*, August 1941; "The Life of Ner Abeline Mazwai, Esq.," Harry Mjamba, *Inkundla ya Bantu*, December 1941). The *Gallery of African Heroes* was transformed in subsequent years into the Three Journalists forum on New African intellectualism, when Jordan K. Ngubane inherited the editorship of *Inkundla ya Bantu* from Govan Mbeki (there may have been other editors between their tenures).

Having received his tutelage in journalism under the guidance of R. V. Selope Thema at the *Bantu World* and under Ngazana Luthuli *at Ilanga lase Natal*, both of which occurred in the late 1930s, it is perhaps fitting that the first journalistic similar project Jordan K. Ngubane undertook in *Inkundla ya Bantu* before assuming the editorship was a Review of the African Press Opinion under the pen name of "Khanyisa" (Enlightener) from July 30, 1942 to January 30, 1943. In this task, he assessed the opinions of African newspapers such as *Imvo Zabantsundu*, *Ilanga lase Natal*, *Bantu World* and other newspapers of lesser importance. This enabled him to develop a comprehensive knowledge of African newspapers as well as of journalistic practice.

When later in his evaluation of R. V. Selope Thema in the "Three Famous African Journalists I Knew" series of 1946 Ngubane developed a thesis that Selope Thema "is one of the greatest sons we the African people have produced" because of his contributions principally in *Umteteli wa Bantu*, and also in *Bantu World*, his assessment was authoritative given the many years of deep engagement with African newspapers, or, for that matter, with South African European newspapers also. That he turned out to be a great journalist in the 1940s, on par with H. I. E. Dhlomo, if not surpassing him, should not be an occasion for surprise.

Ngubane was sharp in his assessment of the quality of some of the newspapers, as is evident in the following comment on *Umteteli wa Bantu*:

> Feature writers of this journal have that knack of writing stimulatingly which that journal's editorials sadly lack. *Umteteli* of all papers read by Africans has lukewarmness in its editorial presentation of the African case which contrasts very strikingly with the more positive approach of such of its capable correspondents as Mrs. Margaret Ballinger and "Gossip Pen." ("Review of African Press Opinion," *Inkundla ya Bantu*. October, 1942)

In the same column, writing of *Imvo Zabantsundu*'s attempt to make sense of the rivalry between the African National Congress and the All-African Convention, he reflected: "Some refreshing commentary on the African home front came from this journal when it turned its searchlight on the cancer of internal dissension and our 'redundant organisation.'"

He argued in *Imvo*, that awakening the nation and rousing political conscious is most healthy, but divisions and competitive spirit among national organisations deprive them of the community's best minds, "that there is no need for parallel organisations." The upshot of these reflections was to become clear in 1944, when upon the assumption of the editorship of *Inkundla ya Bantu*, he effectively made it the intellectual voice of the ANC Youth League. In a letter to the editor of the newspaper the year before, he articulated what he understood to be the responsibility of African newspapers to the New Africans:

> When going through the back numbers of the *Inkundla ya Bantu* I found that this journal was born when times were beginning to be abnormal, and it was not unnatural therefore that when you launched your effort, many entertained anxieties about the prospects before your paper. You are not past the crisis yet, but can look back over the last five years with pride … modest pride, commensurate with your achievements to … date … It is with no pessimistic intentions that I speak of difficult times ahead … difficult times for the African. It is as well that we know that the world has not gone through its worst suffering, for, a down-trodden people has the temptation to concentrate all its energy and thinking on problems of the present, preferring not to worry much over the future …
>
> It is the duty of the Press that caters for African needs to hold constantly before its readers the need for readiness for the morrow. In this regard, the duty has two aspects … first, the duty to the African and secondly, to the European, both regarded as South Africans who must work out their common destiny by agreement … To the African, the Press has an equal and corresponding duty. It has, first and foremost, to educate the African on his true needs, hopes and aspirations and help him make these known to the outside world in a manner to speed their realisation …
>
> The Press must stand for balanced thinking, for in the final reckoning, it is balanced thinking that leads to national liberation; it is balanced thinking that gives rise to the spirit of tolerance, something we need very much even in our own ranks. The Press has before it the duty to educate our people wisely and responsibly for, if their struggle must succeed, sanity must win them to its side and the duty of a good Press is to be the fount of sanity and not the projector of hysterical jargon. ("Birthday Message," *Inkundla ya Bantu* April 20, 1943)

This was the philosophical and ideological perspective he was to pursue for the next eight years as editor of *Inkundla ya Bantu*. The pursuance of this historical vision transformed *Inkundla ya Bantu* into a great newspaper, while making himself into a formidable New African intellectual on its pages. It is not accidental that in October 1946 its circulation reached 7,000, the highest reached by an African-owned political newspaper in South Africa (Les Switzer and Donna Switzer, *The Black Press in South Africa and Lesotho, 1836–1976*, G. K. Hall & Co., Boston, 1979, p. 44).

As already indicated, because of its spatial reach, intellectual content and uncompromising political commitment to African Nationalism, Alfred B. Xuma, then President-General of the ANC, attempted to buy and transform *Inkundla ya Bantu* into an ideological organ of the ANC. Unfortunately he did not succeed. Impressed with the intellectual power of the young Jordan K. Ngubane, then approximately 27 years old, Xuma began consulting with him on critical matters affecting the ANC. In turn, Ngubane brought H. I. E. Dhlomo with him into the inner confidential circle of the organisation. Xuma's awe of Ngubane in all probability emerged from his reading Ngubane's extraordinary critiques of D. D. T. Jabavu's All-African Convention and Paul Mosaka's African Democratic Party, in defence of the ANC ("Exchange of Courtesies in the Bloemfontein" [South African Political Commentary], *Inkundla ya Bantu*, January 17, 1944; "Intellectuals vs Intelligentsia" [South African Political Commentary], *Inkundla ya Bantu*, December 30, 1943).

In inviting H. I. E. Dhlomo to participate in his project of historical appraisal of the attainments of New African intellectuals, Jordan K. Ngubane had been very much conscious of the inestimable value of newspapers in forging African intellectual traditions, which he hoped the analytical powers of his friend would reveal. The analytical powers of "Busy-Bee" were made evident when he evaluated Dhlomo's *Valley Of A Thousand Hills*, in effect an intellectual self-portrait in which, among other things, he noted the following: that Africa's past speaks through Dhlomo; Dhlomo was a poet of vast creative powers; and lastly, in writing this poem, Dhlomo had incarnated himself as the surging inner spirit of the African people (*Valley of A Thousand Hills*: Story of Feeling, Hope and Achievement: Book By Herbert I. E. Dhlomo, *Ilanga lase Natal*, November 29, 1941).

Given that H. I. E. Dhlomo appraised R. V. Selope Thema as a very important journalist, perhaps it is not surprising that Ngubane would select him as one of the three authors for his consideration, guided by his own estimation of him as also a major South African intellectual ("Through *Umteteli*'s Pages: A Review of 1930," H. I. E. Dhlomo, *Umteteli wa Bantu*, January 3, 1931; when R. V. Selope Thema retired as editor of *The Bantu World*, Dhlomo wrote a short notice: "Mr. R. V. Selope Thema Retires From Active Editorship," *Ilanga lase Natal*, August 23, 1952). R.V. Selope Thema's importance was evident from the fact that as editor of *The Bantu World* during the 1930s, he had as editorial assistants R. R. R. Dhlomo, who was to become editor of *Ilanga lase Natal* in 1943, Ngubane himself, who in 1944 became editor of *Inkundla ya Bantu*, and Henry Nxumalo, who became a central voice in *Drum* magazine in the 1950s. Elsewhere we have postulated the thesis that Selope Thema in the 1920s, on the pages on *Umteteli wa Bantu*, was arguably the principal architect in the construction of African modernities in South Africa.

Although the intellectual portrait of Richard Victor Selope Thema was the last in the series of *Three Famous African Journalists I Knew*, and generationally he follows after John L. Dube and Ngazana Luthuli, he will be the first to be considered here because he has had a much greater impact than the other two in defining the intellectual content of the practice of African journalism. The fundamental thesis Ngubane develops concerning Selope Thema is that he betrayed his great genius by being self-satisfied with writing journalistic pieces and being an editor, instead of developing into a national writer wrestling with the intractable problems the Africans were facing in constructing modernity.

In other words, interpreting his dissatisfaction with his greatly-admired mentor, one can argue that he believed very strongly that Selope Thema had wasted his twenty years in the editorship of *Bantu World* by preoccupying himself with its mundane matters, instead of also writing challenging intellectual and artistic works like the New Negro intellectuals such as W. E. B. Du Bois and James Weldon Johnson, who Selope Thema himself admired. Du Bois' editorship of Crisis did not prevent him from undertaking monumental works such as writing *Black Reconstruction* or *The Negro* or *The World and Africa*.

Likewise, Johnson, while in the position of editor of the New York Age, managed to write *The Autobiography of an Ex-Colored Man, Black Man-*

hattan and *God's Trombones*. (To be fair to Selope Thema, he did write an *Autobiography*, perhaps modelled on Booker T. Washington's *Up From Slavery*, which for unknown reasons was never published even though it was already set in the galleys. The only extant copy is at OWAS which unfortunately this author has been unable to gain access to because the library allows only white South African 'scholars' to see it.) Although Jordan Ngubane does not mention these New Negro writers or the United States context, the tone of criticism gives one inference to this; he was well aware that for New African intellectuals, New Negro achievements were the measuring rod, as R. V. Selope Thema himself had written elsewhere:

> But however marvellous this may be, the wonder of wonders to my mind is the progress which the American Negro has made during the fifty years of his emancipation from slavery ... What is themes sage of this progress to us in Africa? What the American Negro has done and is doing we can also do in this sunny land of ours. (R. V. Selope Thema, "Negro Progress in America," *Umteteli wa Bantu*, December 22, 1923)

It was these writings by Selope Thema in *Umteteli wa Bantu* in the 1920s that had the most profound effect on Ngubane:

> His best writings which have come down to us are drawn from the first ten years of Hertzog's rule, when African intellectuals took a leading part in discussing the problems of their people. Certainly, they groused, complained and threatened a lot—but Mr. Thema spent quite a good deal of his time replying white charges against the African.
>
> In the host of intellectuals who influenced our thinking in those times, Mr. Thema was the only one who was as practical as he was realistic in his approach. The haughty white man who, when he set, his foot on South African soil, thought of Africans only as servants and forgot that they were proud people with glorious traditions, made Thema's blood boil. But at the same time he constantly reminded himself and his people that the African ability to use military force against oppression had been destroyed at Ulundi. (Jordan K. Ngubane "Three Famous African Journalists I Knew: III, Richard Victor Selope Thema," *Inkundla ya Bantu*, July Second Fortnight, 1946)

What was particularly interesting and revealing about Ngubane's thoughts on Selope Thema's brilliant journalistic reflections was that while they were insistent on imparting lessons about modernity, Ngubane was equally insistent on transforming them into lessons about African Nationalism. The remarkable thing about this relationship between these two outstanding New African intellectuals was that it symbolically represented the fundamental historical choices the African people were facing: Modernity or anti-Nationalism?

Despite Jordan K. Ngubane's observation that R. V. Selope Thema was "the most unique subject in the history of African journalism," or perhaps because of it, he was wary of what he considered to be debilitating shortcomings engendered by Selope Thema himself having become intellectually self-satisfied with the editorship of *Bantu World*:

> To most people he is … and rightly too … a retiring intellectual giant, who spans the gap between our immediate past and our present. There is no doubt that Mr. Thema possesses one of the finest and most brilliant intellects in our political life today. His writings today certainly reveal very little of the brilliant journalist who made and pulled down Congress Presidents for a quarter of a century. They have lost their virility, nationalistic force and are not, one might add, very convincing. No longer does Mr. Thema write to give a lead; to stir his readers into thinking. He writes merely not to lag behind the main current he, among others, set in motion over thirty years ago. There is neither disintegration nor decadence behind this; but a grievous national tragedy.
>
> Men of Mr. Thema's intellectual strength do not just crumble down into nothing, nor do their thoughts and philosophies fade into the limbo of forgotten things. These men build nations and shape history and live throughout time. I write this to emphasize the depth of the tragedy behind Mr. Thema's watered-down writings. . . To me, Mr. Thema is one of the greatest sons we, the African people, have produced. (Govan Mbeki, "Gallery of African Heroes: Past and Present." *Inkundla ya Bantu*. May, 1941)

An acquaintance with R. V. Selope Thema's writings of the 1920s convinces one of the solidness of this extraordinary judgement by Jordan K. Ngubane. Without a doubt, R. V. Selope Thema's writings in *Umteteli wa Bantu* in the 1920s, those of Solomon T. Plaatje in *Tsala ea Batho* in the 1910s, and those of H. I. E. Dhlomo in *Ilanga lase Natal* in the 1940s are among the highest summits of South African journalism in the twentieth century. They constitute points in the construction of South African modernity.

Ngubane's reflections on John Langalibalele Dube, the first in this series, were more political in orientation, rather than intellectual, as was the case for Selope Thema. Ngubane's portrait written in 1946 a few months after the demise of the first President-General of the ANC. Between the portrait and the death, Ngubane wrote an obituary, which perhaps should be our first concern here. In this tribute, Ngubane emphasises that John Dube took concrete action to actualise his emergence as well as that of the African people from the depths of oppression to full citizenship.

The achievements of the New Negroes, especially of Booker T. Washington for his inspiration and possible attainments, could not be overestimated: "While in the United States he had come in contact with the Negro Press and had learnt to appreciate its potentials as an instrument of mass education" ("John Langalibalele Dube: A Tribute," Jordan K. Ngubane, *Inkundla ya Bantu*, February, First Fortnight, 1946).

In consequence, the founding of Ohlange Institute went hand in hand with the launching of *Ilanga lase Natal*. Both of them were necessitated by pedagogical interests. In matters of journalism proper, Ngubane makes this indisputable and irrefutable judgement: "He did not play a very important part in the literary side of Journalism. Here, he was more of an administrator than anything else."

Dube's journalistic pieces do not leave a memorable stylistic impression, especially when compared to the virtuosic masterpieces of Ngubane himself or H. I. E. Dhlomo or R.V. Selope Thema. This tribute is itself a masterpiece of compression and brevity, yet brimful with provocative and original ideas organically interwoven. Ngubane's political assessment of John Dube is astute: although he strove incessantly for African national unity, and despite the fact that he was chosen as the first General-President of the ANC, his attachments were still more profoundly aligned with tribal societies than fully with African Nationalism.

In other words, in actuality John Langalibalele Dube was still a transitional figure between tradition and modernity, however much he may have perceived himself as a product of modernity. Ngubane finds the proof of his political estimation in Dube's novella, *U-Jeqe: Insalaka Shaka*, in which tradition fascinates and engages his imagination much more strongly than modernity. A careful reading of *Ilanga lase Natal* from its inception in 1901 to 1956, under the editorship of, successively, John Dube, Sikweleti Nyongwana, Ngazana Luthuli, and R. R. R. Dhlomo, ambivalence towards modernity was still very strong despite the contributions of such New African intellectuals as Josiah Mapumulo, Benedict Vilakazi, Pixley ka Isaka Seme, Alfred B. Xuma, H. Selby Msimang, Martin L. Kumalo, and Jordan K. Ngubane in the late 1930s under pseudonym of "Jo the Cow". It were the prodigious and inimitable contributions of H. I. E. Dhlomo to the newspaper under the pseudonyms "X" and "Busy-Bee" and under his own name, under the tutelage of his brother, that brought *Ilanga lase Natal* irreversibly into the modern age.

In his intellectual portrait of John Dube as a journalist, Jordan Ngubane made the same observation as he had a few months earlier in the obituary, that creatively as a journalist he had not contributed and accomplished much. This portrait is memorable for this startling information:

> At one time the proprietors of *Umteteli wa Bantu*, a journal which had been reorganised by its new owners to combat Communism among the Africans ... particularly in the African Territories ... sought the services of John Dube. Thus, for a time he served as editor of this journal. After leaving *Umteteli wa Bantu*, he returned to Natal where he devoted most of his time to building Ohlange Institute. ("Three Famous African Journalists I Knew: I, John Langalibalele Dube," *Inkundla ya Bantu*, Second Fortnight, 1946)

The historians of African newspapers in South Africa confirm this statement with a similar observation: "John L. Dube and Solomon T. Plaatje, both with national reputations as energetic and articulate spokesmen for the African people, appeared as joint editors on the masthead from May to August 1920" (Les Switzer and Donna Switzer, *The Black Press in South Africa and Lesotho*, op. cit., pp. 110–111). Given that the newspaper was inaugurated in May 1920, John Langalibalele Dube's participation in its launch gave him a prominent role in shaping its historical and cultural vision. In fact, it could be argued that, although he was no longer editor of *Umteteli wa Bantu* when the brilliant historical essay of H. Selby Msimang was written and published ("The Religion and Civilisation of the Bantu," September 9, 16, 23, 30, October 7, 1922), a text in all probability influenced in its poetics by Allan Kirkland Soga's "The Hottentots or Khoi-Khoin" (*Izwi la Bantu*, August 20, 27, September 3, 10, 17, 24, October 5, 22, November 5, 12, 1901), its ambivalence toward modernity was more reminiscent of that of Dube and Plaatje than the affirmation of modernity exemplified by R. V. Selope Thema, and which subsequently triumphed on the pages of *Umteteli wa Bantu*. H. I. E. Dhlomo's essays and articles in the newspaper in the late 1920s and early 1930s were no mean measure in facilitating this triumph.

The third journalist Jordan K. Ngubane considered was Ngazana Luthuli. Although hindered by personal friendship from stating openly that the thirty-year stint of Ngazana Luthuli as editor of *Ilanga lase Natal* had not resulted in the greater education and inspiration of the African people, Ngubane attributed this shortcoming, firstly, to the fact that Ngazana Luthuli preferred engaging cultural matters rather than the politics of oppression and domination which had become the central part of the lived experience of Africans. Secondly, since Ngazana Luthuli lacked original ideas and a profound sense of intellectual engagement, despite being a voracious reader, he preferred turning himself into an alto ego of John Dube.

Thirdly, Ngazana Luthuli had developed a defeatist attitude and an feeling of inferiority as a result of the defeat of the African people by British imperialism in 1879 ("Three Famous African Journalists I Knew: II, Ngazana Luthuli," *Inkundla ya Bantu*, July, First Fortnight, 1946). Jordan Ngubane states that African newspaper readers have always asked why John Dube had chosen him for the editorship of the newspaper but, equally puzzling, why had he allowed his reign to last so long. Arguably, the fundamental criticism Jordan Ngubane implicitly made of Ngazana Luthuli was that he never fully and adequately utilised the resources of this great newspaper to forge the unity of African people through African Nationalism. This was the fundamental historical project of Jordan K. Ngubane in the age of modernity in Africa and South African history, as his voluminous unpublished writings in the Carter-Karis Collection testify.

This is what he expected all New African intellectuals to be politically preoccupied with. This may explain the deep-rooted emotional alliance he formed with H. I. E. Dhlomo when the Dhlomo brothers succeeded Ngazana Luthuli in the editorship of *Ilanga lase Natal*. Elsewhere we indicate the extraordinary nature of this intellectual and political alliance between these premier pathfinders of the Zulu Intellectual Renaissance.

In his obituary notice on Pixley ka Isaka Seme in *Inkundla ya Bantu* in 1951, and in political portraits of Allison Wessels George Champion and Albert J. Luthuli for the *Masterpiece in Bronze* series in *Drum* magazine in 1952 and 1953, respectively, Jordan K. Ngubane was defining the New African political intellectual as an African Nationalist. In contrast to these sketches, his brief obituary notice on the death of Benedict Wallet Bambatha Vilakazi in *Inkundla ya Bantu* in 1946 was a portrayal of an African Nationalist as a 'pure intellectual.'

Since Jordan K. Ngubane was himself included in the *Masterpiece in Bronze* series, in an intellectual portrait by A. P. Mda, it is perhaps important to consider how other New African intellectuals viewed him, as invaluable as how he had been viewing other New Africans. Mda emphasises that the intellectual formidableness of Jordan K. Ngubane comes from his combining and synthesising four critical positions: political analyst, scholar, thinker and first-rate journalist ("Jordan Ngubane," *Drum*, May 1954). Although recognising him as a major thinker and brilliant scholar, A. P. Mda views his journalistic contributions as arguably the most important aspect for they constructed the foundations and ideological perspective of African Nationalism.

Already as assistant editor of the *Ilanga lase Natal*, J.K. Ngubane had shown great promise as a writer. His column in *Ilanga* where he wrote under the nom de plume "Jo the Cow" showed his wide reading as well as his rapid development toward maturity. But the flowering of his journalistic genius was to come with the rise of *Inkundla ya Bantu*. Here, he wielded a power which profoundly affected the trend of political history, not only in Natal and the Transvaal, but also throughout South Africa. Once he came out openly in support of African Nationalism, the triumph of that outlook was assured, and it is common knowledge that the emergence of African Nationalism altered the face of politics in South Africa.

Indeed, as has already been noted, and as A. P. Mda authoritatively emphasises, Ngubane not only utilised *Inkundla ya Bantu* as the ideological forum of the ANC Youth League, enabling Anton Lembede and A. P. Mda himself to articulate fully the ideology of African Nationalism, but also as an instrument for destroying Paul Mosaka's African Democratic Party, which had pretensions of rivalling the ANC, as well as bringing about the downfall of Champion as General-President of the Natal ANC. He was instrumental in rallying the ANC Youth League around Albert Luthuli to replace Champion. A. P. Mda writes the rather startling statement that although Ngubane in the 1950s aligned himself with South African Liberalism, he had a certain intellectual sympathy for certain Marxist political categories.

Again, whilst he admired the Marxist ideal of a classless society in which exploitation of man by man will be ended, he nevertheless abhors some of the revolutionary practices and methods of achieving the ideal. By the time of the Interview of 1964 with Gwendolyn Carter in exile in Swaziland, a dialogue which was overshadowed by the consequences of the defeat of African Nationalism at the hands of Afrikaner Nationalism at the Sharpeville Massacre of 1960, a defeat no doubt attributed to the perceived predominance of Marxism rather than African Nationalism within the ANC, Ngubane had reverted to his deep hatred of Communism of the 1940s:

> And I thought him [A. P. Mda] at the time ... and I still think now ... that he was one of the finest political brains produced by my community. Of course the other thing that attracted me to him was his hostility to communism, even at that stage. He took up a very realistic attitude. He felt that it wasn't important for us at that stage to declare war on communists. In this sense we had to expel them from the ANC. We were too weak. If we could use them at that stage to strengthen the ANC we should do so. There were very heavy pressures in the ANC to expel the Communists at that time. The leader of this Anti-Communist crusade was Anton Lembede. ("Interview with Jordan K. Ngubane by Gwendolyn Carter," 5 March 1964, p. 4, Carter-Karis Collection, Center for Research Libraries, University of Chicago)

From this moment onwards until his death in 1985, Jordan K. Ngubane was principally preoccupied with restoring African Nationalism as the primary African political philosophy of modernity.

In his tribute in the form of an obituary to the memory of Pixley ka Isaka Seme, the founder of the ANC in 1912 (then known as the South African Native National Congress), Jordan K. Ngubane underlined his admiration for Seme's unwavering commitment to African Nationalism, as well as for having been the greatest African nation builder in South Africa in the first half of the twentieth century:

> For it is to the vision of Dr. Seme that we are indebted for the unity of the African people ... In the travail that was to come upon all the people, Dr. Seme saw the seeds of the national unity which was dear to him; the unity which, he was convinced would one day establish the African as a free man in the land of his birth ... At that historic conference [the founding moment of the ANC] every African group of consequence was represented. Dr. Seme laid before the representatives of our people the dangers into which we as a people had been thrust.
>
> ... [H]e outlined his vision of the New Africa that would grow out of the travail which awaited them. The people saw the vision and in a moment of unparalleled greatness took one of the most epoch-making decisions ever taken in Africa. They agreed to cease to be narrowly nationalistic; that is, they ceased to be narrowly Zulu or Xhosa or Sotho. They set their eyes on a New Star. They buried the rivalries, jealousies and quarrels of the past and emerged from the conference a New People ... the African People. History records few occasions when New Nations were created so quickly and without bloodshed. That event marked a turning point in the history of South Africa. It was a bloodless revolution and the driving-power behind it was none other than the quietly-spoken and shy Dr. Seme. ("Dr. P. ka I. Seme: A Tribute," *Inkundla ya Bantu*, June 30, 1951)

Although Jordan K. Ngubane seems not to have been familiar with Pixley ka Isaka Seme's great essay of 1905, "The Regeneration of Africa," as a credit to his extraordinary analytical powers, it is amazing that from only evaluating Seme's political praxis in founding the ANC, Ngubane was able to reconstruct the philosophical and political ideology which enabled this momentous event. Essentially, from the practice, he was able to extract the theory of African history in exact correspondence with that formulated in Seme's text, a text which we postulated elsewhere as a founding moment of African theoretical modernity. Clearly, the assembling of the delegates by Pixley ka Isaka Seme that constituted the founding moment of the ANC was one of the greatest events in the making of modernity in South Africa in the twentieth century: the configuration of a New Africa, the making of a New People, the creation of New Nations, and the guidance of the New Star of African Nationalism.

The articles of John Dube written in Mark S. Radebe's *Izwe la Kiti* a few months after this epoch-making event convey this profound historical sense of the newness in the making. In agreement or synchrony with Pixley ka Isaka Seme, Dube was unyielding in his belief that the Africans in tandem with other South Africans must construct modernity:

> The system of tribal segregation may have suited very well a period when barbarism and darkness reigned supreme, and nothing was required beyond those doubtful blessings, but it had and has the fact defect of being essentially opposed to all enlightenment and Christianity, of utterly lacking what nowadays is our supreme requirement ... the power and means of raising the native people out of the slough of ignorance, idleness, poverty, superstition ... in one word, of utter uselessness as citizens or even servants in a civilised land. The times have changed, and manners must change with them. We are in a civilised land to-day, and unless we are to be a burden and menace to it, unless we are to be trampled down in the race forward, we must be enabled or enable ourselves to come up to the scratch and take our place in the running. ("Segregation: The Native View," *Izwe la Kiti*, December 4, 1912; reprinted from *Mercury*)

Given their oppression and domination, the participation of African people in the making of modernity necessitated a political organisation which would concretise their historical vision by overcoming the obstacles and difficulties that were historically imposed by European imperialism and colonialism:

> In my mind it is not to be merely a political organisation, but it is to be a *progressive movement* along all lines of *modern progress*, we ought to appoint standing Committees to carry on the plans for Industrial Education, training in agriculture, sanitation and the developing of a pure home-life. We must

develop native leaders among our young educated people of such breadth and qualities of statesmanship that they may be instrumental in the uplifting of the masses of our people. This to some may seem to be a far look into the future, but in my mind this is our great project and I believe it is that of our esteemed friend P. ka I. Seme, B. A. who convened the first meeting. (John L. Dube, "South African Native Congress", *Izwe la Kiti*, January 1, 1913)

Although paradoxically invoking the exemplary figure of Booker T. Washington who was politically conservative, John Dube was historically conscious of the fact that modernity was by its very nature a progressive movement. The concrete actualisation of this belief in the inseparability of modernity and progressive thought was realised in the founding of *Ilanga lase Natal* and the Ohlange Institute.

Following in the lineage of Pixley ka Isaka Seme and John Dube, Albert Luthuli in the 1940s too subscribed to the philosophical ideology that a New Historical Consciousness must inform the lived experience of Africans. Given that the ANC Youth League was seeking to instil this consciousness in the form of the Programme of Action, and given that Jordan K. Ngubane was himself a principle member of the Youth League, it is not surprising that he would find much in Luthuli that was fascinating. Ngubane's intellectual and political portrait of Albert Luthuli in 1953 on the occasion of the latter's assumption of the presidency of the ANC replacing Dr J. S. Moroka was in many ways bland and unoriginal, in contrast to the very profound psychological portrait he was to write of Luthuli in the early 1960s in the secret *Unpublished Autobiography*, when Ngubane sought to explain why and how white nationalism (Afrikaner Nationalism) had defeated black nationalism (African Nationalism) at the Sharpeville Massacre of 1960.

The marked contrast between the two portraits is perhaps explained by the fact that one was written in celebration of triumph, whereas the other one was penned as an interrogation of history at the moment of defeat and despair. The early portrait merely reiterated the known facts of Luthuli's life history without an original analysis of its historical form (Jordan Ngubane, "Albert Luthuli: President of the Congress," *Masterpiece in Bronze*, February 1953). This portrait was placid and lifeless, and not adding anything at all new to what H. I. E. Dhlomo had already written about Luthuli.

But Ngubane's reflections in *Unpublished Autobiography* by far exceed those of Dhlomo in their brilliance. Those reflections will not be considered here since they fall outside the scope of this essay, which attempts to reconstruct New African intellectual history by means of a particular generic form: sketches of African intellectuals and leaders which appeared in African newspapers that were co-terminous with the historical experience of modernity.

In contrast to the banishment of history in the Luthuli sketch, Jordan Ngubane's portrait of A. W. G. Champion as a political and labour leader was configured within a deeper structure of historical forces (Jordan Ngubane, "A. W. Champion," *Masterpiece in Bronze*, October 1952). Ngubane began by noting that at the moment of the formation of modernity in South Africa in the early part of the twentieth century, white oppression limited the options the Africans had to make something of themselves *inside* South Africa. They could either choose between being a teacher or a clerk; it was impossible be educated to become a doctor or a lawyer or an engineer. This is the reason why African doctors or attorneys in the early part of this decade had to obtain their education and training abroad, either in the United States or in Britain; examples include Pixley ka Isaka Seme, Alfred Mangena, Richard Msimang, and Silas Modiri Molema.

Ngubane traced the historical role of Champion as General-Secretary in the leadership of the Industrial and Commercial Workers, as well as the conflicts he had with its President-General, Clements Kadalie. What is so astonishing about this portrait is that Jordan Ngubane completely ignores Champion's important political role within the ANC, especially within its Natal provincial branch. The conflicts between John Dube and Champion within the Natal African National Congress were legendary. Also legendary were those between Alfred Xuma, then President-General of the national body of the ANC, and Champion, the President-General of the Natal provincial body in the late 1940s.

The reason for the erasure of Champion's political history within the ANC is explained by the fact that in the previous year Ngubane together with H. I. E. Dhlomo as well as the members of the ANC Youth League colluded in destroying his political power base in Natal, replacing him with Albert Luthuli as President-General of the Natal African National Congress. In mentioning only the role of Champion within the labour movement and nothing at all of his political history within the national organisation, Ngubane was in effect 'saying' Champion's political role had been disastrous and destructive. In *Unpublished Autobiography* Ngubane reveals why Dhlomo and himself in their respective columns in *Ilanga lase Natal* and in *Inkundla ya Bantu* made a mutual pact to destroy the political career of A. W. G. Champion. It is nearly impossible to exaggerate the importance of this document.

This portrait of Champion shows the brilliance of Jordan Ngubane as both an intellectual and a journalist. Under the guise of saying that the history of the labour movement will realise his shortcomings, Ngubane was in effect implicitly passing judgement that the history of African Nationalism from the perspective of ANC will be hard pressed to say positive things about him:

> History has decreed that the ICU should not live to see its dream come true. It had made tragic errors of judgment; its leaders had made colossal mistakes for which the movement paid dearly. And none paid more dearly than Messrs. Champion and Kadalie. History will record that Champion suffered more than anyone else, for the punishment was mitigated only for a while, to be inflicted, with cyclonic fury later, when it brought to an end his active political career … History will not forget his solid achievements. If his methods of struggle were often erratic there can be no doubt whatsoever that he had an instinctive and abiding love for liberty and made colossal sacrifices for it. (Jordan K. Ngubane, "Three Famous African Journalists I Knew." *Inkundla ya Bantu*. July second Fortnight 1946)

It is absolutely clear that Dhlomo and Ngubane were absolutely determined, as were many others, to prevent A. W. G. Champion from committing tragic errors and colossal mistakes with the ANC, especially at the moment of the deathly struggle against white nationalism (apartheid) which had made its intentions unmistakeably clear as of 1948: the destruction of African Nationalism. The praise rang hollow because it was made after Champion had been destroyed politically, a destruction from which Champion was never to recover in the remaining approximately two decades of his life. The *Unpublished Autobiography* would say 'openly' in 1963 what, for political reasons, could not be said openly in 1952.

Later in the 1950s as a member of the Liberal Party writing for its newspaper *Contact*, Jordan Ngubane was to shift his intellectual focus onto other matters. The Sharpeville Massacre of 1960 was to bring him back to the question of African Nationalism against Afrikaner Nationalism. After his return in 1980 from a twenty-year exile, Jordan K. Ngubane attempted an intellectual snapshot of the whole New African Movement rather than of its single, individual members (J. K. Ngubane, "40 Years of Black Writing," in *Umhlaba Wethu*, (ed.) Mutloase Mothobi, Skotaville Publishers, Johannesburg, 1987).

Writing from the perspective of attempting to resurrect African Nationalism, which he felt had nearly been destroyed during the 'triumph' of *apartheid*, Ngubane designated Walter Rubusana as the paramount intellectual figure through whom a viable African intellectual history could be reconstructed from a nationalist perspective. In designating Rubusana, Ngubane was seeking to argue that a nationalist intellectual portrait of the African people had to be undertaken from the perspective of the discipline of history. This new position is in marked contrast to that formulated in an editorial nearly forty years earlier in an intellectual portrait of Benedict Vilakazi, whose poetry and scholarship were postulated as at the vanguard of the African people trying to make sense of the historical experience of modernity:

> But his achievements go further than that. While pursuing his studies, Dr. Vilakazi continued to work untiringly to win more respect for the Zulu group and did not spare opportunities that came his way to interpret the Zulu people to the world, whose distinguished son he is. In newspaper articles and public lectures he has done more than any living man to let the world understand Zulu culture better ... Apart from anything else said so far, Dr. Vilakazi is the most outstanding poet the African people have at present. Already, he has published two Zulu poem books and done intensive research into the subject of Zulu Poetry.

> To all these outstanding achievements, he has now added the Doctorate of Literature. We like to emphasize one aspect of Dr. Vilakazi's work in which he has differed from most of our scholars to date; the amount of research he has carried on by himself. He has refused to swallow indiscriminately white misrepresentations of the African and has taken every opportunity to make his own enquiries and as a result has succeeded in bringing to the surface very useful information on the African. Most of our brilliant scholars have been afraid of doing as much research and publishing their findings as Dr. Vilakazi has done ... More than any other living man, Dr. Vilakazi has set an excellent example for our growing generation while his poetic contribution to the advancement of our cause qualifies him for the title of *Imbongi Yesizwe Jikelele*. (J. K. Ngubane, "Dr. Benedict Vilakazi," *Inkundla ya Bantu*, April, First Fortnight, 1946)

Several observations concerning this remarkable passage must be made. It would seem that the research efforts of Benedict Wallet Bambatha Vilakazi were to inspire Jordan Ngubane during his exile to do research on African philosophies with the intent of constructing a metaphysical system of *Ubuntu* for African Nationalism which would thereby make it absolutely resilient in the upcoming struggles against Afrikaner Nationalism.

Secondly, in undertaking this project in exile, Ngubane was to commit the fatal mistake of seeing Zulu Nationalism as interchangeable with African Nationalism. This confusion about the interchangeability of historical objects and processes that have their own distinctive characteristics can already be seen in the passage when Ngubane fails to recognise that arguably Vilakazi was much more concerned and preoccupied with Nguni culture than with Zulu culture per se. Thirdly, one is compelled to dissent from this view of valourising the poetic skills of Vilakazi above those of Dhlomo. The following year, in 1947, in *Ilanga lase Natal*, Dhlomo was to write a series of his great prose poems.

The judgement of Ngubane was predicated on an implicit principle of 'nationalistic evaluation' that, since the poetry of Vilakazi was written in Zulu, it had to be 'superior' to that of Dhlomo written in English; they both utilised the Romantic poetic heritage in different ways. Fourthly, in calling Vilakazi, a national poet, *Imbongi Yesizwe Jikelele*, Ngubane was in effect saying that with the passing of the great Xhosa poet, S. E. K. Mqhayi, the year before, the mantle had been passed on to the Zulu poet. Both Mqhayi and Vilakazi were part of the same Nguni tradition. In an obituary, Jordan Ngubane had this to say of the great poet who left a deep impression on the school boy Nelson Mandela in a High School visit to the Transkei:

> The news of the death of Samuel E. Krune Mqhayi at Ntabozuko has come as a staggering shock on the African people. Mqhayi has been discovered not only to have been an outstanding poet among the Xhosas, but to have been a son of whom the Zulu, Sotho and Shangane were rightly proud. But Mqhayi was also an eminently successful poet. At a time when it was fashionable to look down upon African cultural heritages, Krune Mqhayi became almost the lonely voice in the wilderness singing *Izibongo*. (J. K. Ngubane, "S.E. Krune Mqhayi," *Inkundla ya Bantu*, August 31, 1945)

It would seem that for Ngubane, Mqhayi was not only a national poet, but also a nationalist one. Arguably the triumvirate of H. I. E. Dhlomo, Benedict Wallet Vilakazi and Jordan Ngubane was the most formidable intellectual force in the intellectual history of South Africa in the twentieth century, surpassing that of the intellectuals around *Voorslag*, or those of the Sestigers and, finally, those of the Sophiatown Renaissance.

Ezekiel Mphahlele, as a member of the Sophiatown Renaissance and consequently the third and last generation of New African intellectuals (if we take Pixley ka Isaka Seme and Walter Rubusana to have constituted the first and Jordan Ngubane and H. I. E. Dhlomo to have formed the second), also attempted on his return from a twenty-year exile to construct a synoptic view of South African intellectual and cultural history. Mphahlele's survey is much more scholarly and objective than the one mapped by Jordan Ngubane, since it was based on a better grasp of the extant documentation.

One other central distinction between them was that whereas Mphahlele was more concerned with delineating the narrative structure that informed the Republic of Letters, Ngubane was preoccupied with tracing the philosophical lineage which justifies the necessity of African Nationalism. Similar to the documentation employed in this study written in

1997, Mphahlele's more authoritative effort of nearly a decade ago was also largely based on African newspapers. Another similarity between Mphahlele's project and this author's is that they both get guidance from A. C. Jordan's *Towards an African Literature* (a 1973 compilation of essays which originally appeared in *Africa South* in the 1950s).

Fascinatingly, moving from Tiyo Soga to Keorapetse Kgosotsile emphasised the poetic voices of William Gqoba, S. E. K. Mqhayi and Benedict Wallet Vilakazi. But the real fascination of this intellectual canvas is its location of H. I. E. Dhlomo at its central point. Mphahlele clearly states that Dhlomo created his literary works with a specific intent of reassessing tradition in relation to modernity in order to facilitate the emergence of African Nationalism as a bridging process between the two. This is exactly how Jordan Ngubane assessed Dhlomo's *Valley of a Thousand Hills* when it first appeared approximately forty years before Mphahlele's appraisal of the historical meaning of H. I. E. Dhlomo to South African Letters. Here are some of Mphahlele's brilliant reflections on Dhlomo:

> Herbert Dhlomo went back in history in order consciously to come to terms with the African traditional past that was still alive in his time, whatever damage had already been done. He also believed that African dramatic forms should be used as a source of inspiration. He understood, as his published comments show, the way traditional African drama works that it is [a] religious ritual, expressed in song and dance. He was, on the other hand also a universalist, believing that Hamlet, Job, Joan of Arc, *Nongqause* were common to all races. He also believed that African drama could not grow wholly out of its indigenous roots but needed support from Western modes. Dhlomo insisted that the past could serve African art only when the latter had grasped the present. He observed also that the African predicament ... birth and progress ... affords a rich store of material for drama. He wanted playwrights to dramatize and proclaim African philosophy and history, to dramatize oppression, emancipation and evolution. (Es'kia Mphahlele, "Landmarks," in *Umhlaba Wethu*, op. cit.)

This was an assessment that Benedict Wallet Vilakazi would have in many ways assented to. It is interesting what Ezekiel Mphahlele had to say about the aesthetic duel concerning drama and poetry that took place between Vilakazi and Dhlomo in 1938-9.

Mphahlele's large-scale canvas of the post-exile period was in many ways a continuation of the pre-exile endeavours of the 1950s when the Sophiatown Renaissance writers and intellectuals in *Drum* magazine and in the *Golden City Post* newspaper constructed intellectual portraits of political leaders, writers, musicians and religious figures. When Jordan K. Ngubane's brilliant achievements of the 1940s came to an abrupt end with the collapse of *Inkundla ya Bantu* in 1951, it was this third generation of New Africanism which inherited the mantle. The point of transference was the historical memorialisation of Pixley ka Isaka Seme. As we have seen, the last major portrait Ngubane wrote in 1951 in *Inkundla ya Bantu* was an obituary on this founder of the African National Congress.

Two years later, R. V. Selope Thema, belonging to the second generation of New African intellectuals like Jordan Ngubane, contributed a major appraisal of Pixley ka Isaka Seme in *Drum* magazine (R. V. Selope Thema, "How Congress Began," *Masterpiece in Bronze, Drum*, July 1953). Selope Thema argued that although Pixley ka Isaka Seme was a great historical visionary in seeing that in order for African people to make a transition from tradition to modernity they had to make a profound transformation in their historical consciousness from particularistic, ethnic identification to universalistic, national identification (from ethnic 'nationalism' to African nationalism), as a practical political leader and in the years between 1930 to 1937 as President-General of the ANC, he had been a colossal failure because of his authoritarianism and autocratism.

Despite this particular failure, R. V. Selope Thema made a historical judgement of Seme that was very similar to that which had been made two years earlier by Jordan K. Ngubane: that he was one of the greatest South Africans of the twentieth century:

> In spite of all this, Pixley ka Isaka Seme has made a notable contribution to the development of our consciousness and national spirit, both creative and driving forces in our forward march. He has thus left his mark on our unwritten history, and when this history comes to be written by African historians, his name will certainly find a place of honour among the great men of our race. (A. P. Mda, "Jordan K. Ngubane", *Drum* magazine, May 1954)

It could be said that it was this intellectual and political portrait that gave the Sophiatown Renaissance intellectuals the wherewithal to write South African intellectual history using this generic style. This last generation of the New African intelligentsia, who symbolise the last intellectual snapshot of modernity in South Africa, transformed in very significant ways the cultural scope and cognitive texture of the intellectual essay. Whereas with the first generation we saw Pixley ka Isaka Seme write an appreciation of Walter Rubusana, or with the second generation H. I. E. Dhlomo make an appraisal of Albert Luthuli, in both instances these seem to be isolated individual endeavours. With the Sophiatown Renaissance intelligentsia this discursive practice was undertaken as a generational, historical process.

Their portraits are across generational identifications as well as within their generation. Admittedly, the intellectual content of the portraits constructed by the Sophiatown Renaissance Talented Tenth never approximated the brilliance of the achievements of their immediate predecessors such as A. P. Mda or Jordan Ngubane. The second modification effected by the *Drum* intelligentsia is that their portraits were largely about artists, whereas inevitably the portraits by the first two generations of New Africanism had been about historical figures and political leaders. One need only note here that practically all the biographical contributions by Solomon T. Plaatje to T. D. Mweli Skota's *The African Yearly Register* (1930) were about Chiefs, the very figures H. I. E. Dhlomo had a deep aversion for.

In fact, although there are no attributions given, one can be certain that many of the portraits of the emergent New African intelligentsia were written by Dhlomo. It is not for nothing that Mweli Skota in the Preface to the book wrote the following: "The Editor also wishes to extend his profound thanks to Mr. H. I. E. Dhlomo for information and photographs appearing in the second part of this book ..." (publisher: R. L. & Co. Ltd., Johannesburg, 1930).

While Plaatje and Seme were enamoured with chieftancy, for Selope Thema and Dhlomo it epitomised the very 'barbarism' and 'heathenism' they despised. This distended the nature of Mweli Skota's classic because while Plaatje is pulling toward tradition, Dhlomo is equally pulling in the direction of modernity. The third mutation change realised by the *Drum* intelligentsia was to disengage the portraits from any kind of political discourse, paradoxically, at the very moment the Youth League made the politics of African Nationalism triumphant within the ANC.

Henry Nxumalo was one of the central figures in these transformations. He was, generationally speaking, in a better historical position than any other Sophiatown Renaissance intellectual to appreciate the achievements of the second generation of the New African intelligentsia such as H. I. E. Dhlomo, R. V. Selope Thema, and Jordan K. Ngubane in consolidating a tradition of writing biographical portraits as a means of constructing intellectual history. Given that Henry Nxumalo, like Jordan Ngubane, underwent his journalism apprenticeship in the late 1930s and early 1940s under the guidance of Selope Thema at *Bantu World*, it is not surprising that a portrait by Selope Thema, such as the one on Pixley Seme, would leave a deep impression and imprint on his imagination. In fact, one of the most important portraits ever written by Nxumalo was on his mentor, R. V. Selope Thema. The other biographical portraits that he wrote on figures of the second generation of New Africanism were on Peter Abrahams and D. G. Mtimkulu.

Written at the moment when R. V. Selope Thema had broken away from the ANC to form a 'National-Minded Block in Congress,' and accusing the national organisation of acquiescing to being dominated by 'extremists' and 'Communists,' Henry Nxumalo laments in sadness his intellectual idol's political conservatism, and personal crisis of alcoholism and belief in superstition ("The Most Controversial Man in Black Politics," *Masterpiece in Bronze*, *Drum*, 1953). Though Henry Nxumalo does not say who these 'extremists' were supposed to be, it is clear that he was making reference to the ANC Youth Leaguers such as Nelson Mandela, Oliver Tambo, A. P. Mda, and Anton Lembede, who together persuaded the ANC to adopt the Programme of Action, thereby precipitating the defeat of Dr Alfred Xuma as President-General of the organisation.

The Programme of Action promulgated a positive policy of political action, such as passive resistance and the burning of passes, in opposition to white oppression and apartheid. The 'Communists' in Selope Thema's characterisation were Africans and Europeans and Indians and Coloureds who were at the forefront of the Defiance Campaign of 1952.

By the time of this portrait, R. V. Selope Thema was only a shell of his former intellectual greatness. Henry Nxumalo mentions some of the achievements of Selope Thema, having become the sub-editor of *Abantu-Batho*, the ANC newspaper launched by Pixley ka Isaka Seme in 1913 (from a combination of two previous newspapers). By the time of his death in 1955, much of his historic importance had been forgotten, as can be seen from the supposition that his outstanding achievement had been his membership of the Natives' Representative Council from 1937 to their termination in 1950 (Matthew Nkoana, "The Man Who Fought For Better Race Relations," *Golden City Post*, September 18, 1955).

The greatest achievement of R. V. Selope Thema was undoubtedly his theorisation of South African modernity on the pages of *Umteteli wa Bantu* in the 1920s before resigning to assume the editorship of the newly founded newspaper, *The Bantu World*, Matthew Nkoana mentioned in his obituary that he had had long conversations with R. V. Selope Thema. Judging from the major political essays written in exile in the 1960s for the London-based, exiled, South African magazine, *The New Africa*, in support of the PAC (Pan Africanist Congress) ideological perspectives, he was probably the inheritor of the legacy of the R. V. Selope Thema of the 1940s, whereas Henry Nxumalo inherited that of the 1930s, and Jordan K. Ngubane that of the 1920s. Characteristic of all three of them was the search for the unity of African people through African Nationalism.

Peter Abrahams represented a different historical meaning for Henry Nxumalo. One essential element of the importance of Abrahams for Nxumalo is that he had to leave the country in order to forge and sharpen his modernist sensibility as a writer. Abrahams lived in England from 1939 to 1955 where he discovered the Communist cause which he subsequently abandoned. After abandoning Communism, Peter Abrahams affiliated himself with humanism. This was the question posed by his novel of the 1940s, *Mine Boy*: nationalism or humanism. Nxumalo believes that the émigré experience taught Abrahams that one cannot be a writer through hatred, but only through love.

Reviewing Abrahams' *Return to Goli*, which consisted of his impressions gathered a year before after an absence of thirteen years, Nxumalo perceived such a radical transformation in Abrahams' consciousness that he posed the question of whether Peter Abrahams was still a South African writer:

> When I met Peter here and piloted him round these troubled parts he was indeed a new man. His spirit was no longer that of the lad with whom we once shared the trials and tribulations of the colour bar [segregation] in this country. He was even different from the lad with whom we once shared beers in London's homely pubs seven years back. ("Return to Abrahams," *Drum*, July 1953)

The fundamental merit Nxumalo found in the intellectual work and literary works of Abrahams, which was similar to what H. I. E. Dhlomo had noted seven years earlier in *Ilanga lase Natal*, was Abrahams' national identification of himself as an African, rather than as a Coloured. In this, Dhlomo had postulated the influence of New Negro writers and intellectuals such as W. E. B. Du Bois, Langston Hughes and James Weldon Johnson on the South African New Africa. Dhlomo urged the Coloured people of South Africa to follow this lead. In an unattributed intellectual portrait of Z. K. Matthews, Matthews' acceptance of an invitation to a visiting professorship at Union Theological Seminary in New York for the academic year 1952–53 was hailed as a breakthrough for the African people:

> Although he left South Africa at a time when the African people have embarked on an important political campaign, he has the blessing of the entire African community, for his appointment in America means the recognition of the Africans' abilities and honour to the African people. ("Prof. Z. K. Matthews, *Masterpiece in Bronze*, *Drum*, August 1952).

Implicit in this enthusiasm was the acknowledgement that the relations between the New Africans and the *descendants* of the New Negroes could be strengthened and consolidated. The last intellectual portrait written by

Nxumalo for the lessons it may have for the Sophiatown Renaissance intelligentsia was of Don G. S. Mtimkulu. Nxumalo was anxious to indicate the importance of education in uplifting the people and making it easier for them to enter the historical experience of modernity. Nxumalo marvelled at Mtimkulu's having obtained degrees from Fort Hare, London University and Yale University. (In actual fact Mtimkulu never obtained an M. A. degree from Yale University. This fact was revealed to the author in a personal communication by an administrator at Yale University in early 1997 while attempting to obtain a copy of the purported M. A. thesis. I did manage to obtain those of Z. K. Matthews and Selby Ngcobo.) Nxumalo emphasised Mtimkulu's contribution to New Africanism in South Africa through his stewardship as a principal of both Adams College High School and the Ohlange Institute:

> True patriot that he is at Ohlange Don is doing work of love and has rejected several attractive outside offers in order to stay here. In the seven years of his principalship he has made Ohlange one of the largest, most progressive and most successful black institutions in the country. Today many young Africans holding responsible positions in this country have Ohlange to thank for their skills. ("Don Mtimkuku: He was always first!" *Masterpiece in Bronze, Drum,* August 1955)

Mtimkulu had a deep commitment to the philosophy of education as evident in a speech he gave and the essay he wrote upon his return to South Africa in 1938 from studying abroad. In a speech to the Methodist African Institute, Mtimkulu explored the factors hindering African progress. Like so many other New African intellectuals, the measuring rod for progress was the example of the New Negroes in the context of United States modernity. He emphasised four factors: whereas the New Negroes believed in a 'go-ahead' spirit, were a united people, had permanently organised organisations, and practised efficiency, the New Africans were incapacitated in many of these modernist sensibilities (Anonymous, "Mr. Mtimkulu on Factors Inimical to National Progress," *Ilanga lase Natal,* November 5, 1938). Mtimkulu defined his philosophy of education in the following manner:

> Education can either be a revolutionary or a reactionary force. At its best it combines these two elements, preserving a sort of dynamic equilibrium

which, whilst preserving and passing on the cultural gains of the group, yet encourages and stimulates critical thinking on present day and future problems. He showed in his formulation how white domination had inferiorized African education through stratification of society based on race, as well as making the clash of cultures ... between modernity and tradition ... purposely the driving force of modern society. ("The African and Education," *Ilanga lase Natal*, July 8, 1939)

Arthur Maimane was another member of the Sophiatown Renaissance who wrote a significant intellectual and political portrait of a major figure of the second generation of the New African Talented Tenth. Maimane seeks to indicate that the founding of the Industrial and Commercial Union of Africa in 1919 was a momentous occasion in the political history of South Africa. With its founding, the struggle of the African people against white domination moved forward on several fronts: through labour struggle, political struggle, and intellectual engagement with the shape and meaning of South African history. The resiliency, fortitude and determination of Clements Kadalie synthesised these forms of struggle, which in many epitomised the uniqueness of modernity:

> In dynamic and eloquent Clements Kadalie we had the first African who wielded as much power as European politicians; whose word could sway the political balance ... as the I. C. U. did in helping the Nationalists to win the 1924 elections. (Arthur Maimane, "The Late Clements Kadalie," *Drum*, 1952)

Maimane makes passing criticism of Kadalie in having brought from England William Ballinger as adviser to the I. C. U., which resulted in tragic political consequences. The portrait notes the debilitating struggle within the labour organisation in the 1920s and in the 1930s between Kadalie and A. W. G. Champion, the leader of the strongest provincial chapter of the I. C. U. in the nation. Through blind political ambition, the very trait that made H. I. E. Dhlomo and Jordan Ngubane strongly detest him, Champion constantly sought to use his regional base, at whatever cost, to be a major leader on the national stage. Dhlomo and Ngubane thought he did not possess the qualities necessary in a national leader as exemplified by Alfred Xuma and Albert Luthuli. Other than Can Themba's obituary of Alfred Xuma in the *Golden City Post* a decade later, after these portraits of the second wave of New African intellectuals by the successors came to an end, this third and last wave of New African intellectualism began sketching individuals among themselves as exemplifications of the intellectual project of New Africanism.

Can Themba's obituary portrait of Henry Nxumalo in 1957 was the first in a series. As already indicated, generally speaking, he stood at the median point between the intellectual generation of A.P. Mda, Anton Lembede, Jordan Ngubane and Peter Abrahams, and that of the *Drum* writers, Bob Gosani, Peter Magubane, Lewis Nkosi and Arthur Maimane. Because of his historical location, Nxumalo still embodied in the symbolic self the historical forces that shaped the modernistic contours of New Africanism (Can Themba, "Henry Nxumalo," Masterpiece in Bronze, *Drum*, February 1957). By indicating that Henry Nxumalo had written for the *Pittsburgh Courier* to make more money in the aftermath of the Second World War, Themba was observing a phenomenon so characteristic in the construction of New African modernity: the inescapable influence of New Negro modernity in the forging of African modernistic sensibilities—the imperativeness of the connection between Africa and the African diaspora.

In becoming a foreign correspondent of this New Negro newspaper, Nxumalo was continuing in the footsteps of Allan Kirkland Soga, who in the 1900s submitted special reports to the *Colored American Magazine*, and also in those of Clements Kadalie, who in the 1920s did likewise for A. Philip Randolph's *The Messenger*. By also indicating that Nxumalo arrived at his journalistic forte through his apprenticeship at *Bantu World*, as had been the case with R. R. R. Dhlomo and Jordan Ngubane, and thereafter becoming its sports editor, Can Themba was indirectly mentioning that the intellectual legacy of R. V. Selope Thema was seminal in shaping the modernistic qualities of both the second and the last generations of New Africanism in South Africa. In becoming a first rate investigative journalist for *Drum* magazine, Henry Nxumalo was differentiating himself from his master, Selope Thema, who had been in the 1920s on the pages of *Umteteli wa Bantu* a great synthesiser of world historical experiences and visions within the context of world modernity.

In the intellectual portrait of Ezekiel Mphahlele, Can Themba appraises him as having been deeply conscious of the value of education in and of itself, as well as its central role in opening the pathways of modernity to the African people. The reason for this appraisal was Mphahlele's obtaining of a M. A. degree from the University of South Africa:

> When Ezekiel Mphahlele was capped in Pretoria recently for the M. A. degree, he had travelled a long, sparkling way up the ladder of education, and even now with his head high as noon, he is reaching for the stars. He is going for a doctorate. The stirring story of how Zekes spelled out his spasmodic lessons on the pasture lands of Pietersburg, how he stood watch for the police while his mother purveyed illicit liquor in Marabastad, Pretoria, how he see-sawed between the bottom and the top of the class in Pretoria and Johannesburg, how he sweated at mid-night studies to climb his degrees, and ultimately burst into success ... that story is now a South African classic." (Can Themba, "Zeke Past Bachelor of Arts," *Drum*, September 1957)

To have written this, Themba must have read a portion of Mphahlele's manuscript of the autobiography *Down Second Avenue*, which Mphahlele was working on just a few months before he left for exile in Nigeria, an absence that was to last for two decades.

Ezekiel Mphahlele was among the most sensitive of the New African intelligentsia to the historical role of women in the making and construction of modernity. In this, he follows a certain political and social strand of New African intellectualism: The reactionary and politically conservative John Tengo Jabavu, surprisingly enough, was adamant in his belief that Fort Hare should also educate women as much as men. From the planning stages of the college, Jabavu was in conflict with European missionaries who were opposed to the inclusion of women, and happily the perspective of Jabavu prevailed from the time of the opening of Fort Hare in 1916.

Alfred B. Xuma not only held Charlotte Manye Maxeke in the highest estimation as the paragon of an African woman confronting the challenges of modernity, but he also encouraged his second African American wife, Madie Hall Xuma, to continue the legacy of this great African woman upon her death in 1939. Lastly, H. I. E. Dhlomo also wrote a number of articles and essays in *Umteteli wa Bantu* in the 1920s and in *Ilanga lase Natal* in the 1940s showing the great strides women were making out of their own self-volition. Constructing short portraits of women a year before the death of H. I. E. Dhlomo, Ezekiel Mphahlele observed:

> Yes, a number of African women have achieved great things in their time. Some are well known, others are unsung heroines who work silently like ants, and all that people see is a job well done. They are all the more remarkable when we consider that 20 years ago Africans regarded it a waste of time and money to send a daughter to high school and sheer madness to let her go to university. *They are the product of a new era.* (Ezekiel Mphahlele, "Salute to African Women," *Golden City Post*, April 17, 1955, my emphasis)

The 'new era'—in other words, modernity itself—had transformed the historical consciousness of both New African women and New African men. In the actual instance of Ezekiel Mphahlele himself, one can observe in *Down Second Avenue* the influence of his Aunt Dora and his wife-to-be Rebecca Mphahlele in the transformation of his consciousness. In this salute, Mphahlele celebrates mostly modern women who are doctors, social workers, nurses, and teachers. He emphasises that many of them had degrees either from Fort Hare University or the University of Witwatersrand or the University of Natal. An artist he considers is Emily Motsieloa, a pianist and choir mistress who founded the Merry Black Birds Band, one of the outstanding jazz swing bands of the 1930s. In a separate article, he appraised Lilian Ngoyi, one of the great ANC political leaders of the 1950s, a woman who had a profound effect on other extraordinary South African women who followed in her awake: Helen Joseph, Ellen Kuzwayo, Ruth First, Winnie Madikizela-Mandela and others (Ezekiel Mphahlele, "Lilian Ngoyi.")

In selecting Emily Motsieloa, a second generation New African artist, for mention in the midst of social workers and medical doctors, Ezekiel Mphahlele was indicating something which had been evident to the Sophiatown Renaissance intelligentsia, but which the earlier generations of New African intellectuals had been oblivious to: the central importance of art and entertainment in the construction of South African modernity. Jazz provides an interesting example of the shifting allegiances of New Africans. One of the greatest paradoxes in the making of New African modernity is that because of their affinity for European classical music and virulent hostility to jazz as marabi music, the first two generations of

New African thinkers failed to register that one of the greatest modernisers or doorways to modernity for Africans was provided by a musical form invented by the New Negroes—jazz—an invention brought to the world by the people whom they constantly professed to be emulating.

The hostility of Solomon T. Plaatje, R. R. R. Dhlomo, R. V. Selope Thema, Mark S. Radebe and H. I. E. Dhlomo toward jazz is very notorious, and we have examined it in detail elsewhere ("Trans-Atlantic Connections of the New African Movement," in *Black Modernity: A Discourse in Modernity between United States and South Africa*, [ed.] Ntongela Masilela). Mark S. Radebe, as "X" the music critic in *Umteteli wa Bantu* in the 1930s, wrote in celebration of classical and choral music. And likewise "Aureole," the music critic of *Ilanga lase Natal* in the late 1930s and early 1940s, had the same preoccupations.

One could plausibly argue that the founding of the Eisteddfod music competition by Mark S. Radebe and H I. E. Dhlomo in the late 1930s was an attempt to stem the 'Jes Grewing' of jazz in the cultural texture of modern South Africa (Anonymous [in all probability written by H. I. E. Dhlomo], "The Coming Eisteddfod," *Umteteli wa Bantu*, October 28, 1933). It was only in the 1950s, at the historical moment of the Sophiatown Renaissance, that the Dhlomo brothers, then editors of *Ilanga lase Natal*, allowed the coverage and appreciation of jazz on its pages. By then, jazz had already become the dominant musical form of modernity among New Africans.

Arguably, among the *Drum* writers, Can Themba was more conscious of the centrality of art and and entertainment in modernity. It is possible that Bloke Modisane and Todd Matshikiza were also as equally aware. Dolly Rathebe, Victor Mkize and Todd Matshikiza, tell of Can Themba's portrait of Henry Nxumalo.

Historically and generally, the New African Intellectuals can be classified into periods organised around two intellectual movements: the New African Renaissance (1905–1945) and the Sophiatown Renaissance (1950–1960). Each of these movements, articulating the ideology of New Africanism, was principally preoccupied with the construction of modernity and its possible cultural realisation through modernism in South Africa. They were preceded by the Xhosa Cultural Renaissance (1870–1900). The historical conditions that made it possibility were established by the first modern African intellectual in South Africa, Tiyo Soga (1829–71).

The Sophiatown Renaissance was followed by the Staffrider Literary Generation (1976–1988), whose end was marked by the founding of the Congress of South African Writers in 1988. These four intellectual movements constitute a central component of South African intellectual history in the late nineteenth century and practically the whole cultural breadth of the twentieth century. The coalescing, centrifugal centre of each of these intellectual movements were newspapers, magazines and cultural reviews.

Pre-Xhosa Cultural Renaissance (1857–1871)

Tiyo Soga was the first African to study abroad, specifically, at Glasgow University in Scotland. He was ordained as a minister of the United Presbyterian Church in that city in December 1856. His intellectual formation was shaped by, among others, the works of Washington Irving, Henry Wadsworth Longfellow, Thomas Babington Macaulay, as well as by Boswell's *Life of Johnson*, and above all by John Bunyan's *The Pilgrim's Progress*, the first half of which he translated into Xhosa. When he returned to South Africa in April 1857, he brought back with him a part of modernist, European, intellectual culture. He was the first African to consciously acknowledge the historical tension between tradition and modernity.

His *Journals* indicate a continuous preoccupation with this historically monumental issue which was to preoccupy practically all major African intellectuals in the first half of the twentieth century from Thomas Mofolo through R. V. Selope Thema to H. I. E. Dhlomo. Given his great prescience, it is not surprising that on the publication of the first newspaper among the Xhosa in 1862, *Indaba* (News), Tiyo Soga immediately grasped its great import not only in re-activating a sense of history in the Xhosa nation after their defeat by the Europeans in the frontier wars, but also allowing for a reciprocal discourse between modernity and tradition, rather than just the former dictating to the latter:

> ... a beautiful vessel for preserving the stories, fables, legends, customs, anecdotes and history of the tribes. The activities of a nation are more than cattle, money or food. A subscriber of the journal should preserve the copies of successive editions of *Indaba* and at the end of the year make a bound volume of them. These annual volumes in course of time will become a mine of information and wisdom which will be a precious inheritance for generations of growing children. All is well today.
>
> Our veterans of the Xhosa and Embo people must disgorge all they know. Everything must be imparted to the nation as a whole. Fables must be retold; what was history or legend should be recounted. What has been preserved as traditions should be related ... Let us resurrect our ancestral forebears who bequeathed to us a rich heritage. All anecdotes connected with the life of the nation should be brought to this big cornpit, our national newspaper *Indaba* (The News). ("*Ipepa le-Ndaba Zasekaya*" [A National Newspaper], (*Indaba*, vol. 1 no. 1, August 1862; cited in Donovan Williams' *Umfundisi: A Biography of Tiyo Soga, 1829–1871* Lovedale Press, 1978, p. 98–9)

It was with similar intent that Walter Rubusana and Allan Kirkland Soga founded *Izwi la Bantu* in 1897, that Solomon T. Plaatje established *Tsala ea Becoana* in 1910, that R. V. Selope Thema wrote extraordinary columns in *Umteteli wa Bantu* in the 1920s, that H. I. E. Dhlomo edited *Ilanga lase Natal* in the 1940s, that Jordan K. Ngubane edited *Inkundla ya Bantu* in the 1940s, and that Ezekiel Mphahlele worked as literary editor of *Drum* magazine in the 1950s. The legacy that Tiyo Soga left behind concerning the role of newspapers in shaping a national consciousness has been profound.

To forestall the possibility that Tiyo Soga may falsely be seen as having been a celebrant of tradition, it is necessary to quote the following statement which represents his strongest beliefs: "God had made from creation no race of men mentally and morally superior to other races. They are all equal in these respects; but education, civilisation and the blessings of Christianity have made differences among men" (cited in John Aitken Chalmers' *Tiyo Soga: A Page of South African Mission Work*, Edinburgh and London, 1877, p. 421).

In other words, it was modernity that had enabled Europeans to defeat Africans, and it was this historical instrument or historical process that Africans had to unrelentingly acquire or appropriate. This was the historical logic behind Charlotte Manye Maxeke's determination to study at Wilberforce University in the 1890s, where she became a good friend of W. E. B. Du Bois, then an assistant professor at this institution. She returned to South Africa in 1900 and became one of the nation's greatest apostles of modernity. It was also the conviction of the correctness of this belief on the part of John Langalibalele Dube that enabled him to establish the Ohlange Institute in 1901 and found the *Ilanga lase Natal* newspaper in 1903.

Likewise, Solomon T. Plaatje's publication of *Native Life in South Africa* in 1916, a book analysing the deleterious effects of the Natives Land Act of 1913 on Africans, while a member of the ANC delegation to Her Majesty's Government in London protesting the Act, was part of the necessity to accelerate the acceptance of modernity by Africans. Anton Lembede's launching of the African National Congress Youth League in 1944 with Nelson Mandela, Jordan K Ngubane, A. P. Mda, and others, was part of the same historical logic. H. I. E. Dhlomo's incomparable essays on the pages of *Ilanga lase Natal* in the 1940s and 1950s were a way of restating this profound belief of Tiyo Soga.

The actual, precise configuration of the relationship between tradition and modernity was a source of major disagreement among African intellectuals. While Tiyo Soga, Pixley ka Isaka Seme, John Dube, Solomon T. Plaatje and others believed that Chiefs would be the instrumental agents in the transformation of tradition and its transcendence towards modernity, Albert T. Nzula, H. I. E. Dhlomo and others saw them as the very antithesis of the possibility of the realisation of modernity. While Nzula and Dhlomo were led by their different political perspectives to view this critical matter in the same way, it is essential to point out that for Dhlomo it was through African Nationalism that the African people would achieve modernity, and for Nzula it was through the praxis of Marxism. Different from all these positions, practically all by herself, Charlotte Manye Maxeke postulated that the principal task of modernity was to liberate the African woman from the shackles and constraints of tradition. Education, civilisation, and Christianity were at the centre of the construction of modernity in Africa, or should we say, 'African modernity.'

Tiyo Soga's historical, intellectual and ecclesiastical preoccupations were to establish the historical conditions that facilitated the emergence of the Xhosa Cultural Renaissance. However, the principal figures of this movement Elijah Makiwane, Walter Rubusana, Pambani Jeremiah Mzimba, and John Tengo Jabavu seem to have repressed in their intellectual imagination their great intellectual predecessor, in that he is hardly mentioned in their surviving writings. But a sense of continuity can be traced through the nature of the Western intellectual tradition Tiyo Soga imparted to them. One constant theme in some of the essays of the members of the Renaissance is that for them the central canon of English intellectual tradition consists of Shakespeare, Tennyson, Milton, and the essayist and philosopher, Francis Bacon (see for example: John Tengo Jabavu, "Untitled Editorial," *Imvo Zabantsundu*, January 5, 1885; Elijah Makiwane, "Educated Natives," *Imvo Zabantsundu*, January 26, February 2, 9, 1885).

The question of why Makiwane, Jabavu and others chose this particular selection of the English intellectual canon is clarified upon reading the biographies of Tiyo Soga, for both John Aitken Chalmers and Donovan Williams emphasise that these same masters of the English imagination, including Bunyan and Goldsmith, had been chosen by Tiyo Soga as incomparable figures of English culture. Again in seeking clarification for why Elijah Makiwane, the leading figure or ideologue of the Xhosa Cultural Renaissance, passionately and constantly emphasised the importance of the English language as a vehicle for entrance into modernity (see the above mentioned essay; also, Pambani Jeremiah Mzimba, "Education Among The Natives," *Imvo Zabantsundu*, December 30, 1886), the biography by Donovan Williams is of assistance in showing that Tiyo Soga had a deep love for the English language and English literature (p. 106). This could not be a mere coincidence, for Tiyo Soga and Elijah Makiwane seem to have intensely interacted with each other during the era of the *Indaba* (1862–5) and *Isigidimi sama Xosa* (1870–88) newspapers. (Elijah Makiwane might possibly have read Tiyo Soga, who wrote for the former newspaper under the pseudonym of "Nonjiba Waseluhlangeni" [Dove of the Nation] while a student at Lovedale, and possibly they came to know of each other while Makiwane was editor of the latter newspaper.)

It would seem that it was Elijah Makiwane, President of the Educational Native Association, to which all the members of the Xhosa Cultural Renaissance belonged, who brought the intellectual identifications of Tiyo Soga to this group of African intellectuals, who were the first to concern themselves with the historical implications of modernity for the African people. A third point which indicates affiliations between Tiyo Soga and the leading pathfinders of the Renaissance is that it could not be mere coincidence that he had a love of history and Thomas Macaulay, as his biographers clearly demonstrate, and that the first major intellectual disagreement among the members of the Native Educational Association was over the political implications and the 'historical lessons' for African people in South Africa of George Washington William's *History of the Negro Race in America, 1619–1880* (1883). Lastly, all who have come after him have assented to Tiyo Soga's postulation that education, civilisation and Christianity were the essential ingredients in the formation of African modernity, be it William W. Gqoba or Silas Modiri Molema or Mark S. Radebe, Jr. or A.P. Mda. This is the reason why African intellectual culture in South Africa begins with Tiyo Soga.

It remains to note here why this cultural formation was a Renaissance of sorts rather than a full blown Renaissance as was to occur 70 years later within the structure of South African intellectual history. Erwin Panofsky's magisterial work, *Renaissance and Renascences in Western Art*, offers many points of illumination.

Xhosa Cultural Renaissance (1870–1897)

The beginning of the Xhosa Cultural Renaissance was marked by the founding of the newspaper *Isigijimi sama Xosa* (The Xhosa Messenger, 1870–88) by European missionaries. The principal articulator of newspaper *Imvo Zabantsundu* (African Opinion, 1884-present) launched by John Tengo Jabavu whose belief was that Africans should control the intellectual forums which expressed their historical vision. The intellectuals who contributed to *Imvo Zabantsundu* were members of the Native Educational Association (NEA) as well as affiliates of the Lovedale Literary Society, both of which were located in King Williamstown.

The second association to emerge, *Imbumba Yama Nyama*, with members such as Mesach Pelem and Paul Xiniwe was based in Port Elizabeth. The one extraordinary event of this moment was the founding of the Ethiopian Movement by Mangane Maake Mokone, the establishing of black independent churches in rebellion against the hegemonic European (white) churches. The early manifestations of John Tengo Jabavu's conservatism was displayed through his use of his newspaper to oppose the Ethiopian Movement. This may have partly precipitated the founding of *Izwi la Bantu* (The Voice of the People, 1897–1909) by Walter Rubusana and Allan Kirkland Soga, the former having once been a protégé of John Tengo Jabavu. Although these two critical voices of *Izwi la Bantu* had their beginnings in this era, they play their fundamental historical role in the era of the New African Renaissance. Ironically, John Tengo Jabavu had himself launched his newspaper in opposition to the *Isigijimi sama Xosa*. The major intellectual figures of this era were the following:

- William Wellington Gqoba (1840–1888)
- James Dwane (1848–1916)
- Elijah Makiwane (1850–1928)
- Pambani Jeremiah Mzimba (1850–1911)
- Mangane Maake Mokone (1851–1930)
- John Knox Bokwe (1855–1922)
- Walter B. Rubusana (1858–1936)
- John Tengo Jabavu (1859–1921)
- Meshach Pelem (1859–1936)
- Isaac W. Wauchope (1845–1930)
- William Kobe Ntsikana (1880–1922)
- Paul Xiniwe (1857–1902)
- W. Z. Soga (-)

New African Renaissance (1905–1945)

Although Walter B. Rubusana and Allan Kirkland Soga were the dominant ideological voices among the founding members of *Izwi la Bantu*, the actual founders and first editors of this remarkable newspaper were Nathaniel Cyril Umhalla (or Mhala) and George W. Tyamzashe. It was this newspaper which established the preliminary forms of African political modernity. F. Z. S. Peregrino's newspaper *South African Spectator* (1900–12) became the ideological forum of the Ethiopian Movement and Pan-Africanism both of which advocated a position that African political modernity is realisable when predicated on the struggle for the unity of all black people in the modern world. Solomon T. Plaatje's *Tsala ea Becoana* (The Friend of Bechuana, 1910–12), subsequently changed to *Tsala ea Batho* (The Friend of the People, 1912–15), took part in the construction of African political modernity by seeking to and succeeding in establishing modern intellectual culture in South Africa.

Solomon T. Plaatje published different sections of *Tsala ea Batho* in five languages: English, Tswana, Pedi, Xhosa and Sotho. This unprecedented act seeking to forge unity among different African ethnic groups was in effect an expression of the vision that made the founding of the African National Congress possible. In fact, it was the principal founder of this organisation, Pixley ka Isaka Seme, who marked the launching of the New African Renaissance with the publication of his essay in the Columbia University student newspaper in 1905 while completing his undergraduate studies: "The Regeneration of Africa." The idea of the Regeneration of Africa was first formulated by United States Negro intellectuals of the nineteenth century, Martin Delany and Alexander Cromwell.

This borrowing from Americans by South Africans was to be a constant phenomenon as the twentieth century unfolded. The most astonishing example of this was John Langalibalele Dube founding the Ohlange Institute in 1901 as a tribute to Booker T. Washington's Tuskegee Institute, as well as launching his newspaper *Ilanga lase Natal* (Natal Sun, published presently as *Ilanga*) in 1903 modelled on Washington's own newspaper. The very notion of the New African Renaissance was inspired by the concept of the New Negro Renaissance; even the idea of the New African resembles the idea of the New Negro. In short, South African modernity is inconceivable without the example of United States modernity. The New African Renaissance was the actual making of political and cultural modernity in South Africa. The persistence of the influence of the United States on South Africa throughout the twentieth century is breathtaking. In the 1940s, in his *Ilanga lase Natal* columns, H. I. E. Dhlomo formulated his construct of the New African Talented Tenth influenced by W. E. B. Du Bois' own concept of the New Negro Talented Tenth theorised in 1903. R. V. Selope Thema, in his columns in *Umteteli wa Bantu* in the 1920s, with more consistency and passion than any member of the New African Talented Tenth, was conscious of the historical lessons New Negro modernity had for the construction of New African modernity.

Selope Thema was the chief ideologue from the African perspective in the making of South African modernity. Together with H. I. E. Dhlomo, Solomon T. Plaatje, H. Selby Msimang and Allan Kirkland Soga, R. V. Selope Thema participated in the most spectacular theorising of modernity, on the pages of *Umteteli wa Bantu*. Selope Thema was uncompromising in his belief that modernity should simply vanquish tradition; for him there could possibly be no organic or rational relation between the two. In his long editorship (1932–52) of *Bantu World* from its inception to his retirement, he exhorted Africans to follow the example of African Americans in entering fully into the historical experience of modernity.

The names of R. R. R. Dhlomo, Herbert Isaac Ernest Dhlomo, Benedict Wallet Vilakazi, Anton M. Lembede, A. P. Mda, Jordan K. Ngubane, A. H. E. Made are of the members of the Zulu Intellectual Renaissance (1940–56) which occurred within the historical vision of the New African Renaissance. The renaissance is centrally associated with the name of H. I. E. Dhlomo. The emergence of the Zulu Intellectual Renaissance was marked by two interrelated events: the publication of Dhlomo's epic *Valley Of A Thousand Hills* in 1940, and Jordan Ngubane's immediate literary evaluation of it in *Ilanga lase Natal* as forging a 'modern national spirit.'

The renaissance was consolidated by H. I. E. Dhlomo becoming assistant editor to his brother at *Ilanga lase Natal* in 1943 and by Jordan K. Ngubane at nearly the same time taking over the editorship of *Inkundla ya Bantu* from Govan Mbeki. Dhlomo's new position gave him the opportunity to write his great essays of the 1940s and 1950s in the newspaper. When the ANC Youth League was founded in 1943, Jordan transformed *Inkundla ya Bantu* to become its ideological and intellectual forum.

The extraordinary intellectual friendship between H. I. E. Dhlomo, Jordan K. Ngubane and Benedict Wallet Vilakazi is what gave deep sustenance to the renaissance. The Youth League, with Anton Lembede as the principal ideologue, imparted to *Inkundla ya Bantu* the ideology of African Nationalism. Dhlomo's English plays of the late 1930s, R. R. R. Dhlomo's Zulu historical novels of the 1930s, Made's Zulu essays, and Vilakazi's Zulu novels as well as his great scholarship exemplified by his magnificent dissertation, *The Oral and Written Literature in Nguni*, and the *Zulu-English Dictionary* made it nearly an incomparable episode in the cultural history of South Africa in the twentieth century, far exceeding in intellectual prowess the Sophiatown Renaissance.

H. I. E. Dhlomo's death in 1956, nearly a decade after that of his beloved Benedict Vilakazi, marked the end of this great period. Until his death in 1985, in his brilliant writings, however politically skewed, Jordan K. Ngubane was to provide an illuminating beacon on the magnificent intellectual world he and his colleagues had created decades earlier. Tragically, this intellectual world has been ignored by South African scholarship. Following is a list of the major figures of the New African Renaissence:

- Francis Zaccheus Santiago Peregrino (1851–1919)
- Walter B. Rubusana (1858–1936)
- Allan Kirkland Soga (1862–1938)
- Mohty Mahatma Gandhi (1869–1948)
- John Langalibalele Dube (1871–1946)
- Abdullah Abdurahman (1872–1940)
- Charlotte Manye Maxeke (1874–1939)
- Samuel Edward Krune Mqhayi (1875–1945)
- Thomas Mofolo (1876–1948)
- Solomon T. Plaatje (1879–1932)
- Isaac Bud-M'Belle (1870–1947)
- Alfred Mangena (1879–1924)

- Pixley ka Isaka Seme (1880–1951)
- Richard W. Msimang (1884–1933)
- Davidson Don Tengo Jabavu (1885–1959)
- Richard Victor Selope Thema (1886–1955)
- Henry Selby Msimang (1886–1982)
- Harold Cressy (1889–1916)
- Silas Modiri Molema (1891–1965)
- Albert Luthuli (1898–1967)
- Mark S. Radebe (-)
- Zachariah Keodirelang Matthews (1901–1966)
- R. R. R. Dhlomo (1901–1971)
- Herbert Isaac Ernest Dhlomo (1903–1956)
- Jacob M. Nhlapo (1904–1957)
- Benedict Wallet Vilakazi (1906–1947)
- Archibald Campbell Jordan (1906–1968)
- Helen Joseph (1906–1992)
- Yusuf Dadoo (1909–1983)
- Monty G. M. Naicker (1910–1978)
- Lilian Ngoyi (1911–1980)
- Bennet Makalo Khaketla (1913–2000)
- Ellen Kuzwayo (1914–2006)
- Anton M. Lembede (1914–1947)
- A. P. Mda (1917–1993)
- Jordan K. Ngubane (1917–1985)
- Walter Sisulu (1912–2003)
- Oliver Tambo (1917–1993)
- Nelson Mandela (1918–2013)
- Phyllis Ntantala (1920–1998)
- Peter Rezant (-1998)

Native Marxism and the Labour Movement (1921–1948)

The formation of the Industrial and Commercial Workers' Union of South Africa (I. C. U.), later known as the Industrial and Commercial Workers' Union of Africa, on January 17, 1919 by Clements Kadalie with the assistance of A. W. G. Champion and H. Selby Msimang was a momentous occasion in the unfolding of the New African Renaissance. Coming from present day Malawi, the thinking, alignments and affiliations of Clements Kadalie were similar to those of the New Africans in his new home of South Africa. Like his predecessor, the Ghanaian F. Z. S. Peregrino, Clements Kadalie brought to realisation transatlantic connexions in the context of modernity, which the New African intelligentsia was in the process of consolidating. Placing himself at the forefront of New Africanism, like the other New African intellectuals, he founded a newspaper, *The Workers' Herald*, for the new workers' movement.

Like some other members of the New African Talented Tenth, he was deeply impressed by the achievements of Booker T. Washington. Kadalie wanted to replicate the attainments of this New Negro concerning education, civilisation and Christianity in the whole of Africa through the example of South Africa. Like Allan Kirkland Soga, Clements Kadalie drew a direct link between New Africanism and New Negroism. Just as Soga had been in the years 1903–4 an African correspondent for the *Colored American Magazine*, Kadalie in the years 1923–5 was likewise one for A. Philip Randolph and Chandler Owen's *The Messenger*. In one of his essays, Clements Kadalie notes:

> As we write the whole country is in a political turmoil. Both the I. C. U. and the African National Congress are jointly decided to organize the workers both politically and industrially. The pending struggle in this country is a direct challenge to the British Labour Movement and to International Labour. We shall ask the civilized workers of the world:
>
> Are they to sit idle, giving no assistance to the workers of Africa? Words would fail us to be precise, the space allotted to me in this journal will not permit our indictment of the British Imperialist atrocities in the so-called Dark Continent. We do not intend to fill this page with instances showing the savagery and profanity of this much boosted Empire … If they fail to assist us this way, they would have no justification to exist as a Labour Movement. They shall compel us to join and to echo the narrow and selfish slogan, 'Africa for the Africans,' but because we are reluctant to adopt this slogan, hence our appeal to the British Labour Movement. Let the British Labour Movement lead the way in not only preaching but in practising the glorious doctrine of the Fatherhood of God, the Brotherhood of Man. ("Political Storms in Africa," *The Messenger*, August 1925)

Theorising the Modernist Moment of New African Intellectuals

This affirmation of international workers' solidarity was part of the consolidation of the New African entrance into modernity: The African Native of today is a new man and is therefore quite different from his fore-fathers whom the white man found here some two hundred years ago and they duped. The most peculiar man ever created by Dieu is an African Native. He takes no heed to the white man's mischievous propaganda, he has lost hope in white man's leadership and his religion. To determine to frighten him by writing or otherwise at this juncture is to weld him closer together. ("Black Trade Unionism in Africa," *The Messenger*, November 1924)

Clements Kadalie projected the workers' participation in New Africanism and in the construction of modernity against the philosophy of Marxism, or more specifically, against Bolshevism. In this he had the support of most of the New African intellectuals, as can be seen from these reflections from R. R. R. Dhlomo:

Dear readers, I know by praising the efforts of Kadalie, I am spelling my doom as your friend and acquaintance. Mr. Kadalie, because of his fearless policy of calling a spade a spade has incurred, not only the animosity of the Europeans, but that of his fellow men, who see in Kadalie a bar to their plans of self-aggrandisement and advertisement ... I am sure that I am not the only one who is not a little pleased by the step Mr. Kadalie has taken against his officials who had communistic tendencies. Although we deplore the fact that these men, rather than forsake their communistic tendencies had to risk or face dismissal from the I. C. U. ("Kadalie & Communism," *Ilanga lase Natal*, February 18, 1927)

In contrast to Clements Kadalie, for Albert T. Nzula the very essence of modernity was inconceivable or unrealisable outside the historical purview of Marxism. While for Kadalie, like the majority of New African intellectuals, African Nationalism was to be the ideology of New Africanism, for Nzula it clearly had to be Marxism. Because of these conflicting ideological perspectives within the workers' movement in South Africa, this domain of the making of South African modernity was very contentious. Their conflicting historical positions were reflective of the two institutions which were contesting for the allegiance of the proletariat: the I. C. U. and the South African Communist Party.

Although the South African Communist Party was founded in 1921 as a 'white workers' party', Albert Nzula played a key role in transforming it to align itself with the interests of African workers. His early death at the age of 27 was a great blow to South African intellectual culture that could be compared in its consequence impact to the death of Piero Gobetti within the Italian socialist movement. In bringing Marxism to New Africanism and pitting it against African Nationalism through the inspiration of Lenin's *Imperialism, The Last Stage of Capitalism*, Nzula, in his great essay, "The Struggles of the Negro Toilers in South Africa," written in 1933 but published two years later made a critique of the ANC and the I. C. U., and a brilliant critique it was:

> It was a realization of the weaknesses that arise out of tribal divisions and differences that gave the very first national movement its character of a striving towards the formation of a great Bantu nation united against the Boer imperialists. This movement came under the leadership of the African National Congress founded in 1912, an organization representing the chiefs, headmen, priests, lawyers and other petty bourgeois elements of the Bantu population. By placing its main task as the fight against Boer Imperialism, failing to see or completely ignoring the role of British Imperialism, it played directly into the hands of British bourgeois liberals whose interests were in some respects opposed to those of the Boer semi-feudal land owners. The British bourgeois liberals desired a free labour market and therefore did not consider such measures as the semi-slave pass laws indispensable. In spite of this African National Congress had the overwhelming support of the native peasantry and a large section of the native workers who did not see through their false programme ...
>
> The brains and moving spirit of this organization was Clements Kadalie, himself not a native of South Africa but of East Africa [actually Tanganyika in Central-East Africa, today Malawi], in Cape Town. Kadalie was not uneducated in socialist literature, and this was what gave the I. C. U. a distinct working class bias in spite of the petty bourgeois leadership, as opposed to the nationalist character of the African National Congress. The end of 1924 ushered in a lull in the revolutionary movement. Between then and 1930, the Industrial and Commercial Workers Union developed into a reformist organization under the leadership of the Amsterdam Trade Union International. In 1926, Kadalie, the secretary of the I. C. U., under the pressure of the social-fascists and bourgeois liberals who infested the movement as 'sympathizers' and

'advisers', was persuaded to expel the native and coloured Communists from the organization. From this time on, there was a rapid disintegration of the I. C. U. In July 1928 Kadalie publicly denounced the strike of 18,000 miners on the diamond diggings at Lichtenberg, Transvaal. (*The Negro Worker*, vol. V nos. 2–3, 4, 5, 6, 9, 10, 1935)

Without a doubt, the essay, in its analysis of the practice of Marxism in South Africa, puts this particular praxis on a par with any Marxism practised internationally. Its cogent appraisal of the strikes undertaken by the working class in South Africa in the first thirty years of the twentieth century, including the slightly different Bambatha Rebellion of 1906, reflects the tradition of C. L. R. James' *Pan-African Revolt* (1938), which traces the various rebellions and strikes in the black world since the Haitian Revolution of 1804 as part of that Jacobin tradition. In its will to forge a *native form* of Marxism which is simultaneously international in its orientation and scope, the essay also belongs in the tradition established by Jose Carlos Mariategui's *Seven Interpretive Essays of Peruvian Reality* (1928).

Within a national context, the essay established the form of Marxism which was carried forward by Govan Mbeki in the 1940s and 1950s, and continued in the Exile Period (in the 1960s and 1970s), and by Bernard Makhosozwe Magubane in the 1980s. Albert Nzula's early death was a great and tragic intellectual loss. It is fascinating to think how, in the 1940s, he would have engaged Jordan K. Ngubane, Anton Lembede and H. I. E. Dhlomo representing African Nationalism on the one hand, and I. B. Tabata and A. C. Jordan representing Trotskyism on the other. He has left us a great legacy and an immense task. Some of the major figures of this movement are:

- Allison W. G. Champion (1893–1975)
- Clements Kadalie (1896–1951)
- Albert T. Nzula (1905–1933)
- Moses M. Kotane (1905–1978)
- Isaac Bangani Tabata (1909–1990)
- Yusuf Dadoo (1909–1983)
- Monty G. M. Naicker (1910–1978)
- Govan Mbeki (1910–2001)

- Goolam H. Gool (-1962)
- Ahmed Mohamed Kathrada (1929-)

Sophiatown Renaissance (1950-1960)

There is a direct connection between the Zulu Intellectual Renaissance and the Sophiatown Renaissance in that both H. I. E. Dhlomo and Jordan K. Ngubane contributed creative writing—a lyric and a short story, respectively—to the early issues of *Drum,* a magazine which was to become the intellectual and cultural forum of the Sophiatown Renaissance as the 1950s unfolded. Both of them again wrote profiles for the review of major figures of the New African Renaissance: Dhlomo wrote his most penetrative account, the intellectual profile of Benedict Wallet Vilakazi; and Ngubane scribed a subtly damning political profile of Allison W. G. Champion. The Sophiatown Renaissance can be linked to the New African Renaissance in another way: in that the major African journalist on the pages of *Drum* magazine, Henry Nxumalo, undertook his apprenticeship under the guidance of R. V. Selope Thema when the latter was the editor of *Bantu World.*

The Sophiatown Renaissance was the culminating episode in the making of modernity in South Africa, the historical experience which the preceding intellectual and cultural movements had been preoccupied with creating. The most astonishing thing about the Sophiatown Renaissance is the breathtaking audacity it had in attempting to replicate the cultural texture and achievements of the Harlem Renaissance.

Whereas in preceding movements individual figures had appropriated particular African American constructs of modernity—R.V. Selope Thema calling his autobiographical essay "Up From Barbarism" in homage to Booker T. Washington's *Up From Slavery,* or Dhlomo calling for the creation of the New African Talented Tenth in emulation of W. E. B. Du Bois' idea of the New Negro Talented Tenth, or John Langalibalele Dube founding the Ohlange Institute as a tribute to Washington's Tuskegee Institute, or Pixley ka Isaka Seme appropriating and re-articulating the notion of "The Regeneration of Africa" which had originally been formulated by Martin Delany and Alexander Cromwell, or Peter Abrahams' modelling of the naturalistic style of *Mine Boy* on that of Richard Wright's *Native Son*—in contrast to these daring individualistic efforts, the last episode of the cultural, modernistic experience in South Africa attempted to appropriate a whole cultural movement.

Given this utopian gesture, it is perhaps not surprising that the Sophiatown Renaissance has the reputation of having been the most intoxicating moment in our cultural history, hence its extravagant hold on the cultural imagination of South Africans. Although today this cultural moment is lauded for its literary attainments, its real everlasting achievements may turn out to have been in photography and music. With the destruction of the Sophiatown Renaissance at the Sharpeville Massacre of 1960, modernity and modernism bade a terrifying farewell to Africans in South Africa. Thereafter it lived as a ghostly spectre in the political imagination of Europeans. The important literary figures of the Sophiatown Renaissance were the following:

- Henry Nxumalo (1918–1957)
- Ezekiel Mphahlele (1919–2008)
- William 'Bloke' Modisane (1923–1986)
- Can Themba (1924–1968)
- Arthur Maimane (1932–2005)
- Lewis Nkosi (1936–2010)
- Bessie Head (1937–1986)
- Nathaniel Nakasa (1937–1965)

The Outstanding Figures in Photography

- Gopal Naransamy (1927–)
- G. R. Naidoo (1928–1982)
- Jürgen Schadeberg (1931–)
- Peter Magubane (1932–)
- Bob Gosani (1934–1972)
- Lionel Oostendorp (-)

The Outstanding Figures in the Domain of Music

- Manhattan Brothers (1940s–1950s)
- Kippie Moeketsi (1926–1983)
- Dolly Rathebe (1928–2004)
- Miriam Makeba (1932–2008)
- Hugh Masekela (1939–)

Part Two

African Intellectuals and the Development of African Political Thought in the Twentieth Century

Mbukeni Herbert Mnguni[1]

> *The problem of the twentieth century is the problem of the color line, the question of how far differences of race, which show themselves chiefly in the color of the skin and the texture of the hair, are going to be made, hereafter, the basis of denying to over half the world the right of sharing to their utmost ability the opportunities and privileges of modern civilization.*
> W. E. B. Du Bois, cited in Milfred C. Fierce, *The Pan-African Idea in the United States 1900–1919*, 1993, p. 201.

The twentieth century will be remembered as an age in which the colonized peoples—the majority of mankind—asserted their demands for independence. To appreciate this statement fully one has to understand the reality of colonization in depth—its cultural, political and economic implications. One has indeed to

---

[1] Mbukeni Herbert Mnguni is an independent writer. He is currently a member of the Interdisciplinary Center for Historical Anthropology at the Free University Berlin/Germany. He studied Mass Communication at the Centre for Communication Education Studies at Trinity and All Saints' Colleges in Leeds/England. He received his Ed.D. from California Coast University, Santa Ana, USA. He earned his Ph.D. from the Free University Berlin/Germany. His dissertation *Education as a Social Institution and Ideological Process: From a Négritude Education in Senegal to Bantu Education in South Africa*, was published by Waxmann Verlag, Münster, Germany. His published books: *Multikulturelle Bildung: Ein unmöglicher Traum für Südafrika?* (Waxmann Verlag, (2011), Münster, Germany). *Hubani Mabutho kaZulu* (Shuter & Shooter, Pietermaritzburg, South Africa). *Izinkondlo njengosikompilo Nomhlahlandlela Wolwazi* (Poetry as Culture and Theory), (Maskew Miller Longman Press, Johannesburg, South Africa). Essays: 'The Impossiblity of Identity,' *Paragrana*. Internationale Zeitschrift für Historische Anthropologie. Band 9: 2000: Heft 1., Prof. Dr. Gunter Gebauer & Prof. Dr. Christoph Wulf (eds.), Akademie Verlag, Freie Universität Berlin. 'Reaffirming Critical Multicultural Teacher Educational Policy in South Africa,' in *European Studies in Education* (Prof. Dr. Christoph Wulf (ed.), Waxmann Verlag, Münster. 'Der Zulu Schilftanz,' *Paragrana*. Internationale Zeitschrift für Historische Anthropologie, 2012, Akademie Verlag, Freie Universität Berlin. He is currently engaged in a research project on the topic 'Towards a Synthesis of the Oral and Written Text: A Reading of Three Zulu Children's Play Games.'

go beyond these categories and ask the question: when is man a man, or what is man like, devoid of his definition of himself?
Mazisi Kunene, "Introduction" to Aimé Césaire's *Return to My Native Land*, 1969, p. 7.

Introduction

The development of a specifically African Political Thought in the sense of a theory seeking to articulate the movement of political and economic structures in their full complexity is a product of the convergence of various factors and influences: historically, the moment had arrived in which African intellectuals and African peoples forged a unity in order to oppose capitalism, colonialism and imperialism through various national liberation struggles; ideologically, a system of thought or practice was necessary in order to theorise the nature of opposition and resistance, hence the importance of Pan-Africanism, African Nationalism, African Socialism etc.; sociologically, in many African countries there was a profound fracturing in the social structure, whether between the urban and rural spheres, between the Africans and the white settlers, between the peasantry and the then emerging working class, or between the so-called Third World countries and the imperial European countries. In short, the various forms of African Political Thought are a product of history seeking to illuminate the nature and structure of African history. Since African political and historical structures were and still are subordinated to European political and historical structures, it was inevitable that the patterns of African Political Thought would supersede national boundaries and attempt to align itself with internationalism, whatever the difficulties involved in this (Mnguni, 1987).

It was a particular assemblage of African intellectuals who developed the theoretical instruments used to structure the co-ordinates and determinants of the subjects under discussion of African Political Thought in the twentieth century. Though these intellectuals emerged at a particular historical moment, they were representatives of various generations. Included among these intellectuals were W. E. B. Du Bois, Frantz Fanon, Eduardo Mondlane, Kwame Nkrumah, Amilcar Cabral, Leopold Sedar

Senghor, Marcus Garvey, Steve Biko, C. L. R. James, Julius Nyerere, Nelson Mandela, Albert Luthuli, Oliver Tambo and many others. Within themselves as a group they represented different intellectual systems: Pan-Africanism, the African National Congress (ANC), the Black Consciousness Movement (BCM), African Nationalism, African Marxism, African Socialism, Negritude, etc. But the most important of them all (in that it gave birth to and facilitated the development of other African intellectual systems) was Pan-Africanism. The importance of this political philosophy, in so far as it brought about the renewal and resurgence of the African political genius, can never be over-estimated, though paradoxically it was born outside Africa through the active participation of African-American and West Indian intellectuals.

The relationship of these African intellectuals to the then dominant colonial political structures is as equally important as the theoretical coordinates of the African Political Thought which they were then articulating. Antonio Gramsci, the Italian political theorist and brilliant philosopher, in his great book, *The Prison Notebooks*, made a distinction between two conceptual categories of intellectuals: the traditional intellectuals and the organic intellectuals. Whereas the former are attached to, and identify with, the dominant and ruling classes within a country (hence defending their theoretical and philosophical interests), the latter align themselves with the aims, aspirations and ideals of the emerging social classes and oppressed social and ethnic groups. Gramsci defined this phenomenon as a universal process. In his book *The Modern Prince and Other Writings* Gramsci writes:

> Every social class, coming into existence on the original basis of an essential function in the world of economic production, creates with itself, organically, one or more groups of intellectuals who give it homogeneity and conciseness of its function ... in the economic ... social and political field ...
>
> It can be seen that the 'organic' intellectuals which each new class creates within itself and elaborates in its own progressive development are for the most part 'specialisations' of partial aspects of the primitive activity of the new social type which the new class has brought to light. (Antonio Gramsci, 1967, p. 118)

In the African context, during the struggle against classical colonialism and imperialism, most African intellectuals could be classified as belonging to Gramsci's second category. They identified themselves with the oppressed masses and struggled for the liberation of their countries. Since the emergence of the era of neo-colonialism, coterminous with the attainment of independence by our countries, there has also emerged a group of African intellectuals who are traditional and align themselves with the ruling national bourgeoisie and the *camprador* class: whereas Ngugi wa Thiong'o is an organic intellectual identifying himself with the common people, Ali Mazrui is a traditional intellectual whose scholarly works and theoretical writings have defended the interests of the oppressive ruling classes. For more than twenty years Ali Mazrui has portrayed himself as a pro-capitalist and pro-imperialist, which has made him a prominent black scholar in America but fortunately not so much in Africa. His recent television interview about Africa is proof of the deleterious consequences his way of thinking on African intellectual tradition. We hope that one day it would be possible for young African scholars to investigate the nihilism and philistinism of Mazrui's intellectual production in details.

One of the many significant aspects of Frantz Fanon's great book, *The Wretched of the Earth*, is that he examines and situates the evolution of African intellectuals within African political structures. Fanon distinguishes three phases through which the former seem to pass before attaining their true historical calling: assimilation; questioning or rebellion; and national identification or the struggle for national liberation. Each of these phases is determined by complex economic, political, social and cultural factors and processes.

In the assimilation phase, these people completely identify with colonialist or imperialist oppression. Not only are they indifferent to their rich national cultures, they even deny its very existence and that of African history itself. They see themselves as Europeans rather than as Africans. A classic example of this phenomenon was the Senegalese Blaise Diagne who was, for many years, a Deputy in the French National Assembly before the Second World War.

He recruited African soldiers for the French army. Unfortunately those African soldiers who fell on European battlefield are scarcely mentioned in French history, despite being responsible for stopping the marauding German forces at the Battle of the Marne in July 1918. It is not surprising that Blaise Diagne extolled the virtues of French colonialism in Africa (Fierce, 1993, pp. 210–212). It is also not surprising that this period produced nobody or anything of intellectual quality and lasting effect. Frank Wallerstein was probably right when he observed:

> This colonial and class structure establishes very well defined class interests for the dominant sector of the bourgeoisie. Using government cabinets and other instruments of the state, the bourgeoisie produces a *policy of underdevelopment* in the economic, social and political life of the 'nation' and the people ... (Frank Wallerstein, quoted by Anthony Brewer in *Marxist Theories of Imperialism: A Critical Survey*, 1980, p. 162).

The Pan-Africanism Movement

The second phase, which is characterized by African intellectuals questioning colonialist assumptions about our societies and cultural systems, did produce outstanding intellectuals like Aimé Césaire, Leon Damas and Leopold Sedar Senghor, and gave birth to the Negritude movement. Certain strains of African Nationalism belong within it also. It is during this phase, when African intellectuals and the people formed a historical unity that expelled classic colonialism and imperialism, that the great development of African Political Thought took place. It is here that the political philosophies of Frantz Fanon, Amilcar Cabral and Kwame Nkrumah grew to great efflorescence.

Since it was the ideology and the philosophy of Pan-Africanism which precipitated the emergence and development of the various strands of our subject African Political Thought in the twentieth century, it is necessary to pause for a moment and examine the former's intellectual structure and processes. As already indicated, Pan-Africanism as a philosophy developed in the United States and West Indies and it could only have developed and consolidated its theoretical structure there because its principal aim was a historical identification with Africa and, in the process, to assist in bringing about her liberation. Its leading exponents were Edward Wilmot Blyden (Trinidad), W. E. B. Du Bois (United States of America), C. L. R. James (Trinidad) and Marcus Garvey (Jamaica), among others.

Several scholarly works published recently have given different interpretations as to the structure and political aims of the Pan-African Movement but, for our purposes, its main thrusts were the following: to bring about cultural, historical and political identification between Africans and Blacks in the Diaspora (United States, the West Indies and Latin-America); to forge the political means by which Africa could be liberated from colonialist and imperialist domination; to revive and solidify African national cultural systems, which had been traumatised by different colonial imperial forces; and to aim for the possible unification of our continent. The Movement could be said to have been important from the late nineteenth to approximately the middle of the twentieth century.

In his book *The Pan-African Idea in the United States 1900–1919*, Milfred Fierce argues that

> One important manifestation of the early twentieth century interest was an immediate increase in the number of the African-American intellectuals who felt the need to come to Africa's aid.
>
> ... the opening of Black educational institutions of Africans, the providing of technical assistance and African-American assistance in the development of the African national consciousness and Pan-African, among Black American contributions to Africa. (Fierce, 1993, pp. 30, 39)

The transition of the political ideology of Pan-Africanism, or more appropriately, its transplantation and transference from the Diaspora to the African continent, also took place in the second phase, and the direct influence of Dr W. E. B. Du Bois on Kwame Nkrumah was crucial. This transition was symbolised by the Pan-African Congress of 1945 in Manchester, England. Among the many resolutions and declarations, perhaps the following should be noted because of its historical significance:

... that African peoples should take their destiny into their own hands; that the colonial countries should forcefully free themselves from imperialist economic and political domination; that all the peasants and workers and the intellectuals should forge a unity with the aim of expelling colonialism and imperialism from the African continent. (Cited in Robert Chrisman and Nathan Hare, 1974, p. 306)

A Pan-Africanist felt that

[t]he Manchester Pan-African Congress truly marks a turning point in the history of the Pan-African Movement. The turning point consists neither in the unequivocal manner in which the delegates expressed their desire for independence nor in the hostile tone in which the desire was voiced. [Rather], unequivocal demands for freedom and harsh criticisms derived further impetus from the Atlantic Charter, the temporary collapse of the British empire in the Far East and the anti-colonial utterances of several leading American citizens of the day, notably Wendell Wilkie. (Quoted in Chuba Okadigbo, 1987, p. 46)

It was with these declarations that Kwame Nkrumah sought to establish the politics of Pan-Africanism on the continent. On becoming the first President of Ghana, he sought to forge patterns of possible unification and to struggle ceaselessly against all forms of neo-colonialism. On the cultural plane, he attempted to concretise the concept of 'African Personality' which he had derived from Blyden. Nkrumah felt that the revitalisation of our cultural systems would solidify the political structures which could support a united continent.

African Nationalism, which also falls within the second phase, was never important as an intellectual political system, but rather as a political force of mobilisation and liberation. In fact, it was the real historical force which mobilised the masses in the struggle against colonialism and neo-colonialism. But when one looks at the writings of Kenneth Kaunda, Nnamdi Azikiwe, Tom Mboya, Ndabaningi Sithole, and other nationalists, they leave much to be desired. They lack originality, cogency and solid, intellectual content. The reason may lay in the fact that, by the time nationalist ideology had percolated into Africa from Europe, it already had its raison d'être (in other words, it had already exhausted its conceptual categories and historical constructs). Nor is it surprising that these men, on attaining political leadership, never exemplified the political integrity and moral fibre possessed by the late Samora Machel, Julius Nyerere, etc.

The Collapse of Pan-Africanism

The collapse of Pan-Africanism was not caused by the African people, as some writers tend to argue, nor an individual African scholar; it was caused by its failure to introduce a practical and psychological programme which could deal with the economic, including the proper distribution of land, cultural, political, and language problems imposed by the material and political interests of the former colonialists. The Movement failed to create an explanatory model which could integrate psychological needs, such as the fundamental need for identity and self-esteem among the young Africans. It failed to tangle the ethnic 'historicism' which has now resulted in the emergence of wars in Africa. Ntongela Masilela writes:

> The greatest triumph of Classical Pan-Africanism came in 1960, when nearly half of the countries on the African continent attained their political independence. This victory was an outcome of a century-long political and cultural struggle. Yet paradoxically, at the very moment of its greatest triumph Classical Pan-Africanism suffered its fatal defeat, which was to destroy the political legitimacy of this philosophy on the African continent. This defeat was the Congo Crisis of 1960–61, which resulted in three things: the murder of the great African patriot, Patrice Lumumba, whom Jean-Paul Sartre was to memorialize as a 'Black Jacobin and as a revolutionary without a revolution …' This crisis was also the signal that classical colonialism has assumed a new form that of neocolonialism, which was even more vicious than its predecessor. (Masilela, 1994, p. 309)

Kwame Nkrumah's book *Neo-colonialism: The Last Stage of Imperialism* was a political response to the Congo Crisis. It was also written as a historical obituary to the failure of Pan-Africanist philosophy (Nkrumah, 1965).

The collapse of Pan-Africanism and the contradictions that followed helped the former colonialists to re-group and create new strategies to maintain their presence in Africa. Institutions such as the Commonwealth and Francophone were established to advance the so-called friendly ties and mutual assistance, and other forms of cooperation with the former colonies. In his remarkable book *Detained: A Writer's Prison Diary* Ngugi wa Thiong'o elucidates this point when he remarks: "[T]he major contradictions in the Third World is between national identity and imperialist domination. This to me is still the real and fundamental conflict of cultures: viz, a national patrioc culture arising out of and getting its character from the struggle against imperialism. Other contradictions, between the urban and the rural, the modern and the traditional, and between the different nationalities are secondary and they can only be properly appreciated within the context of the larger basic contradiction." (Ngugi wa Thiong'o, 1981)

Furthermore, the structural changes which the decolonisation process initiated were different and as such evoked different responses as the policy folded. It became evident that African states were 'underdeveloped' according to the highly stratified international order. As Professor Galtung put it, two of the most glaring facts about this world are

> the tremendous inequality, within and between nations, in almost all aspects of human living conditions, including the power to decide over those living conditions; and the resistance of this inequality to change. (cf. J. Galtung, "A Structural Theory of Imperialism," in *Peace Research*, 1970, p. 81)

These contradictions also created a smouldering discontent among the masses in Africa which was translated into the language of the radical demands made by the new educated 'riffraff' who portrayed themselves as Africa's second liberators. In other words, the Pan-Africanist's mission was mainly to mobilise the oppressed and the landless to resist colonialism, but after the liberation there seemed to have been no ideas for dealing with the colonial under-development. Addressing the Sixth Pan-African Congress at Dar es Salaam in Tanzania, Sékou Touré recognised the fact that Pan-Africanism had failed the peoples of Africa:

> Pan-Africanism was founded as a serious movement of revolt of a people against the forces of exploitation, aggression and alienation ... Since revo-

lutionary Pan-Africanism basically refers to an Africa of Peoples, it is in its interest to uphold the primacy of peoples as against States ...

Pan-Africanism must first and foremost fight all that tends to confine us to a parochial identity, the identity characteristic of zoos with its history, economy, culture, conception of the sciences, all confined to itself. Such parochialism is likely to lead to very disastrous *stagnation*. (quoted by Chuba Okadigbo, 1986, p. 52)

What Sékou Touré was actually saying was that the power and philosophy of the Pan-African movement lies with the people, not with their political leaders. This was the main political philosophy of the founding fathers of this Movement. Milfred Fierce is probably right when he writes:

Pan-Africanism has been an evolving ideology that encouraged uncertainty. Part of the problem in the past has been the failure to make distinctions between the idea and the movement. (Fierce, 1993)

Witness the following excerpt from Fanon:

In a short time this continent will be liberated. For my part, the deeper I enter into the cultures and political circles of Africa, the surer I become that the great danger that threatens Africa is the absence of ideology. (Fanon, 1970, p. 196)

In his essay, "*The Weapon of Theory*," Amilcar Cabral (1994) argues that "[t]he ideological" deficiency, not to say the total lack of ideology, within the national liberation movements—which is basically due to ignorance of the historical reality which these movements claim to transform—constitutes one of the greatest weaknesses of our struggle against imperialism, if not the greatest weakness of all.

As we can see, with the attaining of independence by many African countries and the contradictions that followed, the immediate, political relevance of Pan-Africanism seemed to have exhausted itself and it was up to other politico-intellectual systems to carry further its aims and aspirations.

The Négritude Movement

In other words, the first phase of our political history never produced any intellectual thought of quality or novelty. It was only with the emergence of the Négritude Movement in the fourth phase that something of real distinction connected with Africa surfaced. Two observations concerning the former have to be immediately stated: firstly, though it was predominantly a literary movement, it did have profound political implications for the African continent; and secondly, to a large extent, it was a product of West Indian intellectuals like Aimé Césaire and Leon Damas, though Africans like Leopold Sedar Senghor and Birago Diop did also participate.

These African intellectuals and writers sought to establish the empirical, scientific basis for their assertion that the future liberation of black cultures in Africa and elsewhere cannot be achieved solely through armed struggle, but must also be effected through the interplay of scientifically-grounded intellectual, literary, artistic and cultural means. Thus, before the 2nd International Congress of Black Writers and Artists held in Rome in 1959, Aimé Césaire stated:

> Yes, ultimately it is the duty of the poets, the artists, the writers, and of all those involved in cultural production to preserve and sustain memory as well as hope in a daily existence of suffering and deprivation of liberty, to raise those magnificent stores of faith, to fill those wonderful reservoirs of strength from which in their moment of need the people may draw the courage to be themselves and bend the future to their own needs. I would remind you that the struggle against colonialism is not to be terminated as quickly as is commonly believed and not merely because imperialism has been defeated on a military level. (Aimé Césaire, quoted in James Arnold, 1981, pp. 37–44)

A recent, excellent study of this Movement indicates that there were several currents within it, the most major being the historical poetics of Césaire and the romantic metaphysics of Leopold Sedar Senghor. Whilst the first sought to establish the historical structures and patterns of African cultural traditions, the second was attempting to theorise the racial ideology of Négritude, which was in many ways historically untenable. Senghor has been severely criticised by many African intellectuals and writers including Wole Soyinka, the first African Nobel Laureate in Literature, and the very distinguished South African writer and scholar Ezekiel Mphahlele (Mnguni, 2008, p. 56).

For Senghor, Négritude was a philosophy of Humanism theorised from the biological constructs of Negro essence. Senghor defended this position by saying that Négritude is "a weapon of defence and attack and inspiration." Because of this, "[i]t is the sum total of the values of the Civilization of the African world" (Leopold Sedar Senghor, quoted in Obi Oguejiofor, 2009, p. 94).

Senghor's definition of the Négritude philosophy could not be in more marked contrast to the historical poeticism of Césaire's Négritude:

> I do not in the slightest believe in biological permanence, but I believe in culture. My negritude has a ground. It is a fact that there is a black culture: it is historical, there is nothing biological about it. I am for negritude from a literary point of view and as a personal ethic, but I am against an ideology founded on negritude ... it seemed to me that Senghor made a kind of metaphysics out of negritude into an essentialism as though there were a black essence, a black soul, ... but I never accepted this point of view. (Aimé Césaire, quoted in James Arnold, 1981, pp. 37, 44)

Ezekiel Mphahlele recognised the historical importance of the Négritude ideology in arousing *protest* among the oppressed people throughout the world, but he felt that the Movement contained some form of segregation and paternalism. He furiously attacked its proponents for romanticising and oversimplifying the African culture and African history. He thought that the Movement told only a small part of the African story and even that half was often a misrepresentation of the reality (Mnguni, 2009, p. 20). Mphahlele vehemently protested:

> Who is stupid as to deny the historical fact of Negritude as both protest and a positive assertion of African cultural values? All this is valid. What I do not accept is the way in which too much of the poetry inspired by it romanticizes Africa as a symbol of innocence, purity and artless primitiveness. I feel insulted when some people imply that Africa is not also a violent continent. I am a violent person, and proud of it, because it is often a healthy human state of mind; some day I'm going to plunder, rape, set things on fire; I'm going to cut

someone's throat; I'm going to subvert a government; I'm going to organize a coup d'état; yes, I'm going to oppress my own people; I'm going to hunt down the rich fat black men who bully the small weak black men and destroy them; I'm going to become a capitalist, and woe to all who cross my path or who want to be my servants or chauffeurs and so on; I'm going to lead a breakaway church—there is money in it; I'm going to attack the black bourgeoisie while I cultivate a garden, rear dogs and parrots; listen to jazz and classics, read "culture" and so on. Yes, I'm also going to organize a strike. Don't you know that sometimes I kill to the rhythm of drums and cut the sinews of babies to cure it of paralysis. (Ezekiel Mphahlele, "Remarks on Negritude." *African Writing Today.* 1967, pp. 247–253)

Mphahlele angrily asked,

Must the educated African from abroad come back to re-colonize us? Must he walk about with his mouth open, startled by the beauty of African women, by the black man's 'heightened sensitivity'? It's all so embarrassing! (Mphahlele, ibid., pp. 247–253)

Further on Mphahlele stated:

It is significant that it is not the African in British-settled territories—a product of 'indirect rule' and one that has been left in his cultural habitat—who readily reaches out his traditional past. It is rather the assimilated African, who has absorbed French culture, who is now passionately waiting to recapture his past. In his poetry, he extols his ancestors, ancestral masks, African wood carving and bronze art, and tries to recover the mornings of his oral literature; he clearly feels he has come to a dead end in European culture, and is still not really accepted as an organic part of French society, for all the assimilation he has been through. As a result, French-speaking African nationalist have become a personification of this strong revulsion, even though some of them have married French women. (Mphahlele, ibid., pp. 247–253)

There is no doubt that Mphahlele was responding to Senghor's book *Senghor: Prose and Poetry* (1965). However, this vitriolic attack on Senghor's Négritude philosophy by a man of Mphahlele's standing was challenged by a number of African scholars and writers including Lewis Nkosi, also a prominent South African scholar and writer. In his book, *Home and Exile and Other Selections* (2006), Nkosi starts by acknowledging Mphahlele's contribution to the debate on the Négritude intellectual Movement, but feels that Mphahlele's aggressive attitude towards the Movement is very weak and lacks the political depth which its founders were attempting to construct. Nkosi accuses Mphahlele for failing to understand the contrary character of the Négritude Movement which contained both positive and negative elements towards European culture (Ntongela Masilela, 1986, p. 7). Mphahlele responded by saying that

> Négritude poetry did not touch the hearts and minds of the masses and, therefore, it taught them nothing, although its architects were using African culture and history. Negritude poetry was produced only for the elite who could read and understand European languages, but not for the illiterate. Such expressions like "Negro-African style" *were merely the concern of a small number of French-speaking Africans who were assimilated into European culture and not the masses.* The assimilated Africans were trapped between African and French cultures. (my emphasis) (Mphahlele, ibid., pp. 247–253)

Bernard Fonlon, an experienced observer of these violent clashes, put it in the following manner:

> The quarrel, if I can call it that, between the French-speaking African and the English-speaking African on the subject of Negritude, stems from the difference in the colonial regimes to which they were subjected ... Mr Mphahlele holds that no South African would deny the historical fact of Negritude as protest, nor would he undermine the importance of this role. But he maintains that in South Africa, they are fighting, not for their Negroness, but for their human dignity. With regard to the role of Negritude as a literary expression, he rejects the view that because a man is black he will write like other black men; all Africans are not the same and therefore Négritude cannot be held up as an ideal prescription for all cultural ills in Africa. (Bernard Fonlon, 2008, p. 20)

On the other hand, Wole Soyinka joined the band of African intellectuals who were severely attacking the Negritude ideology. Soyinka called this intellectual movement a 'Tigritude.'

> A tiger does not shout its tigritude: it pounces. A tiger in the jungle does not say: I am a tiger. Only on passing the tiger's hunting ground and finding the skeleton of a gazelle do we feel the place abound with tigritude, "a narcissistic cult of the African world." (Soyinka, *An Image of Africa*, 1976; see also Soyinka, *The Burden of Memory*, 1998)

It was also with the intent of criticising this attempted construction of the metaphysics and ideology of Négritude by Senghor that Frantz Fanon in *Black Skin, White Masks* wrote sarcastically that the European creates the Negro and the Negro in the state of oppression constructs the philosophy of Négritude. But even more paradoxical here is that Jean-Paul Sartre in *Orphée Noir*, in an introductory essay to Leopold Sedar Senghor's anthology of Négritude poetry, argued convincingly against the danger of constructing the philosophical essentialism of Négritude, the very undertaking the very same Senghor was to pursue with misguided vigour in the years following the publication of this anthology (see Ntongela Masilela, 1986). Jean-Paul Sartre, the French exponent of modern Existentialist philosophy, wrote that

> Négritude appears as the weak link of a dialectical progression: the theoretical and practical affirmation of white supremacy is the thesis; the position of Négritude as antithetical value is the moment of negativity. But this negation moment is not sufficient in itself, and the blacks who employ it well know it; they know that it seems to promise the way for the synthesis or the realization of the human society without racism. Thus Négritude is dedicated to its own destruction, it is passage and not objective, means and not the ultimate goal. (Jean-Paul Sartre, 1947, p. 15)

Fanon did not totally agree with Sartre's attempt to situate the poetics of Négritude within the progression of the dialectic. Fanon thought Sartre was "destroying the black zeal" (Rene Wadlow, 2006; see also Nick Nesbitt, 2010).

On the other side of these arguments and counter-arguments, there were younger and more radical African intellectuals such as Yambo Ouologuem who rejected the Négritude movement in very strong terms, comparing it to "a statue of a hundred myths, a marketplace of fanciful concepts where traders in ideologies list their imaginations on a stock exchange" (Ouologuem, 1988, p. 124). Paul Niger felt that he

> had lived an unreal Négritude, made out of the theories of ethnologists, sociologists, and other scholars who studied man under glass. They have injected the *Negroite* with formaldehyde, and pretended it was a type of happy man. (1978, p. 210, emphasis in original)

Celucien Joseph defended the philosophy of the Négritude movement, commenting:

> Négritude as an intellectual movement provided a sophisticated way of thinking about continental Africa and blacks in the world. This school of thought affirmed unconditionally the valorization of a single African cultural system. (2010)

According to Nesbitt, "[p]olitically, Négritude meant defeating the external factors that defined the Black man physically and psychologically—colonialism and white domination" (Nesbitt, 2010, p. 15).

It would seem that Senghor had drawn his inspiration from a number of sources including the works of the French philosopher Teilhard de Chardin, the Belgian missionary Temples, the German ethnologist Frobenius, as well as from major European thinkers such as Goethe, Marx and Sartre and from a close study of the traditions of African oral literature. Such bicephalism—one may apply the term here in its literal sense—gives the distinct impression that African modes of thought and perception have been subsumed into larger European categories (see L.S. Senghor, "Pierre Teilhard de Chardin et la politique africaine," in *Senghor: Prose and Poetry*, pp. 99–101).

Hans-George Gadamer is probably right when he observes that "[u]nderstanding becomes a special task only when misunderstanding have arisen" (Serequeberhan, 1994, p. 6).

The effect of Césaire's work has been to encourage the search for authenticity and originality in the cultural sphere as much as in the political sphere. However, the concrete example of the fruitful influence of Négritude on the emerging variant of African Political Thought can be seen in its influence on Fanon which spurred him latter on to greater things (Mnguni, 1986).

The National Liberation Movements

The fifth phase which has contributed to the development of African Political Thought in the twentieth century is that of national liberation struggles. This phase is characterised by a fusion of the political theory of intellectuals, thinkers and leaders, with the political practice of the masses (mainly workers and peasants). The target of these struggles was colonialism, whether English, French, Portuguese or Spanish. The outstanding intellectual figures of this era were Fanon, Cabral, Sékou Touré and Mondlane. Nkrumah also belonged to this group but in a tangential way. For the purposes of this article, the most compelling figures are Fanon and Cabral.

In *The Wretched of the Earth*, which has become the classic text of African political theory, Fanon argues that colonialism can ultimately only be defeated through armed struggle. He argues even further that through revolutionary violence the oppressed and the colonised can overcome the inferiority complexes implanted in them by colonialism. This aspect of Fanon's theory has proved to be very controversial up to present times. For example, within American culture, Fanon's view was contested by many intellectuals such as Hannah Arendt who in her book *On Violence* (1994) argued vehemently against Fanon's theory of revolutionary violence. Fanon responded by systematising the philosophy of revolutionary violence:

> [P]sychologically, violence is a cleansing force; historically, the war of liberation, introduces into each man's consciousness the idea of a common cause, of a national destiny and of a collective history; and organizationally, the practice of violence binds them together as a whole, since each individual forms a violent link in the great chain. (quoted by Cedric J. Robinson, 1987, p. 37)

There can be no doubt that Frantz Fanon devoted his life to the Algerian Revolution. He saw himself as a part of the Algerian Revolutionary struggle against French colonialism. This can be seen in his friend's copy of *A Dying Colonialism* where he wrote the following:

> This book is the illustration of a principle: action is incoherent agitation if it does not serve to reconstruct the consciousness of an individual. The Algerian

people, in the great struggle that they lead against colonial oppression, bring to light their own national consciousness so that an Algerian nation, based on mass participation, can no longer be deferred. Have confidence in your people and devote yourself to helping them re-establish their dignity and spiritual awareness. For us, there can be no other choice ... (Fanon cited in Peter Geismar, 1971, pp. 125–126)

Frantz Fanon concluded his book with the following observation:

> The Revolution in depth, the true one, precisely because it changes man and renews society, has reached an advanced stage. This oxygen which creates and shapes a new humanity—this, too, is the Algerian Revolution. (Fanon, *ibid.*, p. 160)

In contrast to Arendt's postulations, for Latin American intellectuals and artists such as the Cuban Roberto Fernandez Retamar and the Argentinian Octavio Getino, the importance of *The Wretched of the Earth* was in its implacable hostility to all forms of neo-colonialism and imperialism, and in its support for the Cuban revolution. In Europe on the other hand, Fanon's book was situated within an intellectual context which also included Professor Herbert Marcuse's *One Dimensional Man* and Regis Derby's *Revolution in the Revolution?* To the Student Movement of the 1960s, for whom these books were sacred political texts, the central issue was not only to oppose America's intervention in Vietnam, but also to establish concrete pathways and patterns of internationalism (see Ntongela Masilela, 1987).

But, as Fanon was a psychiatrist and psychoanalyst, his argument is understandable. His real contribution to African Political Thought was to argue that in the colonial context and also in the Third World in general, the peasantry is the revolutionary class, and not the working class as Marxist theory had postulated. This was because he felt that the working class had been privileged by colonialism. He has been severely criticised for holding this view by many intellectuals, including Cabral, who argues that the peasant class is the *leading physical force* (in so far as the armed struggle depends on their participation) but the working class is the *leading historical force* because it has the capacity and the means of bringing about social, political and economic transformation (Mnguni, 1992, p. 200).

The other major contribution of Fanon was to argue for the indissolubility of political and cultural spheres, hence the two major essays on culture which he presented at the First and Second Conferences of Negro Writers and Artists in Paris in 1956 and the Second which took place in Rome in 1959, respectively. The first essay, "Racism and Culture," which is a critique of the European destruction of African cultural patterns, is included in *Toward the African Revolution*. Most of the other essays in this book are on the Algerian Revolution of which Frantz Fanon was the principal ideologue.

It was through his involvement in this revolution that Frantz Fanon was able to determine the objective coordinates that were essential for Africa's unity and progress in a culture of nations. Equally, it was in this inferno that Fanon felt the need to establish the rudimentary, theoretical constructs and philosophical presuppositions of an African revolutionary philosophy. This crucible made it possible for him to move beyond Negritude and Existentialism towards positioning himself in relation to Marxism, that system of thought which Sartre in *Search for a Method* characterised as "the one philosophy of our time which we cannot go beyond." (Sartre, 1964, pp. 7–8)

One of Fanon's lasting contributions to the development and consolidation of African Political Thought was his critique of the role of the national bourgeoisie in Third World countries. He felt that this class had betrayed its calling by aligning itself with the European bourgeoisie against the interests of its own people. In short, it facilitated exploitation. He equally felt that the national bourgeoisie lacked originality and was profoundly imitative of its European masters. It neglected the development of the countryside and failed in constructing solid, infrastructural supports which would assist development and growth.

The concluding pages of *The Wretched of the Earth* are a passionate and lyrical call for Africa to defend her uniqueness while contributing something original to world culture and civilisation. Indeed, the contribution of Fanon is deep and lasting. Whilst his contribution was made in the relationship between politics and history, that of Cabral was made between culture and history. Their intensive investigations of African history binds them together in developing many pathways through which many of Africa's dilemmas could be resolved. As can be seen from Amilcar Cabral's indirect critique of Fanon, he was much closer to the Marxist tradition. Among his many insightful contributions to African Political Thought, the following passage indicates the originality of this outstanding thinker:

> Whatever may be the ideological or idealistic characteristics of cultural expression, culture is an essential element of the history of a people. Culture is, perhaps, the product of a plant. Like history, or because it is history, culture has as its material base the level of the productive forces and the mode of production. (Almicar Cabral, in the "Weapon of Theory," 1969)

For Cabral, culture, in all its multiple and complex forms, interpenetrates the historical mode rather than merely reflecting it. It is perhaps in this sense that he has been compared to Gramsci. But much more important is Cabral's theory that through armed national liberation struggle the African masses would re-enter the domain of history from which they had previously been expelled by imperialism and colonialism. Not only would they re-enter history but they would take possession of the continent. He had a deeper knowledge of the social structures of practically all African countries than any thinker or intellectual who has ever had the opportunity to reflect on the dilemmas besetting Africa. Because of this, his thought is logical, consistent and systematic in an original way which has never been attained by anyone else. It is therefore not surprising and no accident that his social philosophy and political theory have had a profound influence in many parts of the world. The political thought of Fanon and Cabral both converged towards Marxism, though each in its own particular way.

What we have been considering so far is a tradition of political thought which constitutes the central theme of African Political Thought in the twentieth century. It ought to be observed that, simultaneously with this tradition, there developed a radical theory which was located within the structures of various Communist parties which emerged in the early part of the twentieth century in a few of our African countries. Because of various complications and suppressions, this radical theory never found a congenial home in the different African political structures. Perhaps it was too new and radical for it to be harmoniously assimilated within the confines of the development of the African continent.

The major political theories and systems which we have been considering so far to a large extent pre-date the independence of many African countries, for some they were crucial components of their road to independence. The theoretical constructs and the philosophical concepts of Pan-Africanism, Negritude and African Nationalism were largely forged and propelled by the contradictions existing between the imperial-colonial countries and the colonised nations. The one major political theory of African Political Thought which post-dates the other intellectual systems is that of African Socialism, which came into being because of the internal contradictions that developed in the African countries after independence Frantz Fanon observed that

> [t]he concrete problem we find ourselves up against is not that of a choice, cost what may, between socialism and capitalism as they have been defined by men of other continents and of other ages. Of course we know that the capitalist regime, in so far as it is a way of life, cannot leave us free to perform our work at home, nor our duty in the world ... On the other hand, the choice of a socialist regime, a regime which is completely oriented towards the people as a whole and based on the principle that man is the most precious of all possessions will allow us to go forward more harmoniously. (Fanon, 1967, p. 78)

Although there have been many theories on this subject ranging from that of Tom Mboya to that of Kenneth Kaunda, it is only the African Socialism of Julius Nyerere which merits historical consideration. What has to be said firstly is that he formulated its theoretical system in conscious opposition to Historical Materialism (Marxism) and because he felt that Scientific Socialism did not fundamentally address the problems facing Africa. Secondly, he thought that Marxism had concepts and structures which were incapable of grasping the complexity of African political reality and history. Thirdly, African Socialism was to Nyerere merely an extension within a new historical situation of the communal socialism which had existed from time immemorial and that this would hopefully construct a different doctrine (in contrast to that constructed by Historical Materialism) which would be harmonious with African cultural systems, political patterns, economic processes and intellectual traditions.

In a series of books, including *Freedom and Unity* and *Freedom and Socialism*, he attempted to construct the theoretical postulates and the historical forms of this doctrine and, even more crucially, he implemented it to guide the development of Tanzania. The former's theoretical consistency and historical validity as postulated and practised by Nyerere is a crucial issue beyond our immediate concern. It only remains to be stated that the true realisations of African Socialism in Tanzania encountered many serious difficulties but this was also true of Historical Materialism in Eastern Europe. Mwalimu Nyerere has admitted that the spectacular collapse of *Ujamaa* socialism in his country was not only a national matter but the concern of the whole African continent:

> We set out, in the Arusha Declaration (1967), to build a socialist and self-reliant country. Is Tanzania now socialist and self-reliant? And the answer is "now," it is not socialist; it is not self-reliant. What is it now? This is 1985. I never expected that in 18 years a backward country, which started its independence, as I said, almost totally illiterate, was going to be socialist and self-reliant. (President Julius Nyerere, in conversation with Darcus Howe and Tariq Ali. *Race Today Publications*. March 1986, p. 7)

It was also the existence of certain post-independence contradictions that persuaded Nkrumah to shift his political perspective from Pan-Africanism towards Historical Materialism. This shift was also influenced by the Congo Crisis of 1960–1961 when that great son of Africa, Patrice Lumumba, lost his life. In many ways, Nkrumah's movement towards Marxism coincided with his overthrow in 1966. The first work which indicated this shift was *Neo-Colonialism: The Last Stage of Imperialism* which was followed immediately by a philosophically abstract work entitled *Consciencism*; indeed, a paradoxical continuity.

In subsequent writings (exemplified by *The Class Struggle in Africa*) he deepened his understanding of Marxism and sought to employ its historical and sociological perspectives to resolve some of the problems besetting Africa. He attempted to analyse the interpenetration of class and ethnic structures. Though he never carried his thinking to a conclusion, what he left behind was a solid tradition. It was at this point that the perspectives of Nkrumah, Fanon and Cabral converged towards each other in their historical encounter with Marxism and they sought to make it applicable to the African context.

Nelson Mandela and Steve Bantu Biko: Two Great African Intellectuals

Given the present historical situation in Africa, it is clear that it is in South Africa that African Political Thought had undergone the most remarkable changes. This is, in a way, not surprising, for it is in this country that some of the most complex contradictions on the African continent are most intractable. African Political Thought within the particular context of South Africa shows its own peculiarities. To better grasp the uniqueness of African Political Thought in this context, it is advisable to look, even if only schematically, at two outstanding South African intellectuals who are also great political leaders: "Nelson Mandela" and "Steve Biko." Nelson Mandela served a twenty plus years prison sentence, having been incarcerated by the former, white, South African political state for struggling for a democratic South Africa, and later became the first black President of a multiracial South Africa. Steve Biko was assassinated by the white South African political state approximately a decade ago for struggling for a new, democratic South Africa. Both of these outstanding figures are prominent members of African intellectual culture.

The importance of Steve Biko within African Political Thought partly lies in the fact that he was an outcome of the confluence of the influences of Frantz Fanon, Aimé Césaire and the African American Political Movement of the 1960s. That Steve Biko was a great intellectual figure of our time is confirmed and given credence by many scholarly works. Donald Woods, in adulation of this great son of our country, writes:

> Steve was brilliant. With him you had a remarkable sense of being in the presence of a great mind. Strangely, the word 'clever' did not suit him. He never indulged in intellectual gymnastics for show. His mind was simply a tool to chisel out sense and truth and order. (Donald Woods, *BIKO*, 1978, p. 94)

Steve Biko was a strong proponent of Black Theology. It is for this reason that he directed most of his anger towards the early white missionaries in South Africa, who, according to him, presented a false image of God to the African people:

> Knowing how religious the African people were the missionaries stepped up their terrorist campaign on the emotions of the people with their detailed accounts of eternal burning, the gnashing of teeth and grinding of bone.
>
> Their arrogance and their monopoly on truth, beauty and moral judgement taught them to despise customs and traditions and to seek to infuse into these societies their own new values. (Steve Biko, "Black Consciousness and the Quest for a True Humanity," in *Black Theology*, University Christian Movement, 1972)

For Steve Biko, the concept of Black Theology depicts a God that is for the oppressed and always with them. Biko denounced the hypocrisy of white Christians who pray on Sunday and on Monday aid and abet the *apartheid* system which dehumanised African people (Paula B. Washington, 1980, p. 51).

The political ideas that later distinguished Steve Biko as a heavyweight amongst African intellectuals were forged as early as 1966 when he was a medical student in Durban. In 1969 he was elected the first President of the South African Students' Organisation, an all-black student body. After his expulsion from the medical school because of his political activities, he was central to the formation of the first Black Consciousness political organisation, the Black People's Convention. He was the main co-ordinator of self-help agencies like the Black Community Programmes (see also "Spirits of Biko" in *AWA-FINNABA* (Vusi Mchunu & Mbukeni Herbert Mnguni, eds., 1987).

On the other hand, Nelson Mandela is a great historical force reflecting the influence of Kwame Nkrumah, W. E. B. Du Bois and the African Political Movements of the 1940s and 1950s. Both of these colossal figures are/were brilliant political leaders: Biko was a founder of the Black Consciousness Movement (BCM), and Nelson Mandela was the President of the African National Congress (ANC). It is the very nature of the influences on these two figures that clearly indicates their position within an international Black Political Thought in the twentieth century. In a sense, they can be seen as a continuation of African Political Thought. Although both of their perspectives are unquestionably predicated on the question of the liberation of the black people of South Africa, Mandela's political thought is centred around the question of political freedom as clearly indicated by the argumentation and exposition articulated in his book, *No Easy Walk to Freedom*, while Biko's political thought revolves around the question of cultural consciousness which is clearly formulated in his book, *I Write What I Like*. Ntongela Masilela (1986) writes:

> Biko's book, *I Write What I Like*, is one of our outstanding national books that we South Africans possess in which a rich international African intellectual tradition is brought to bear on our historical experience with tremendous effectiveness. Effectiveness, in the sense of casting a penetrative gaze on our situation, not in the sense of presenting correct historical solutions. (Ntongela Masilela, 1986, p. 20)

In arguing for the autonomy of Black Consciousness, Biko felt himself to be a continuator of the intellectual tradition in South Africa. He saw himself as an extension of the ideology which was central to the African National Congress Youth League. It is perhaps this perceived historical connection that made Biko absolutely certain of his correctness. He felt that the radicalness of the Youth League was responsible for the Defiance Campaign of 1952. However, the real, serious limitation of Biko is that he examined ideology only as a racial category and never as a class relation.

There is no doubt that the contrast between Nelson Mandela and Steve Biko could be made even clearer. While Biko called for black unity through cultural processes of identification and solidarity, Nelson Mandela called for the unity of all the peoples of South Africa on the level of political praxis. It should be made clear that these different perspectives aimed at establishing a democratic South Africa do not necessarily contradict each other. Nelson Mandela's call for political praxis assumes the cultural unity with diversity among African peoples, which Steve Biko saw as the essential preparatory stage. Similarly, Biko's ultimate aim was the very political unity which Nelson Mandela was in the process of enlarging, expanding and deepening. In fact, the different emphases of Mandela and Biko were different stages of the same process of political attainment, namely, the establishing of a democratic order in South Africa, or, for that matter, for the whole continent of Africa.

Their differences may partly be accounted for by the different historical circumstances and conditions of their intellectual formation. The context of the intellectual formation of Nelson Mandela in the African National Congress Youth League was determined by two central factors: the Pan-African vision of unifying Africa, and the contribution of the South African Communist Party to the liberation struggle of the peoples of South Africa.

On the other hand, Biko was deeply influenced by the failure of white classical liberalism to confront seriously the *apartheid* state, and also by the possibility that cultural unity can be a political force that can overthrow a political state. That Steve Biko was disappointed by the white liberals in South Africa can be seen in this statement:

> They [whites] vacillate between the two words, verbalising all the complaints of the blacks beautifully while skilfully extracting what suits them from the exclusive pool of white privileges. (Steve Biko, *I Write What I Like*, 1978a)

It must not be forgotten that Biko equally always worked for reconciliation and mutual understanding between all the peoples of South Africa. For example, he was fond of quoting Aimé Césaire's statement that "no race possesses the monopoly of truth, intelligence, force and there is room for all of us at the rendezvous of victory" (Steve Biko, 1978b, p. 13). In fact, "At the Rendezvous of Victory" is the title of C. L. R. James's collection of essays, a way of remembering both Césaire and Biko.

It must be remembered that Steve Biko came to the political scene at a time when all the political forces of opposition to the *apartheid* state (the African National Congress, Pan-Africanist Congress, the South African Communist Party, the South African Indian Congress, the South African Coloured Congress, the South African Congress of Trade Union, etc.) had been banned and were working underground.

On the other hand, Nelson Mandela's political organisation had forged a political unity, known as the Congress of the People, which brought forth the *Freedom Charter*. The *Freedom Charter*, it was thought, would establish the political doctrine and form of the unity of the people of South Africa. However, for some African South Africans the *Freedom Charter* has become a burden because it gives the white settlers "our land."

Conclusion

In conclusion, therefore, the difference in emphasis in the intellectual and political perspectives of Nelson Mandela and Steve Biko was a reflection of the complex nature of the situation confronting the intelligentsia in South Africa. Nelson Mandela and Steve Biko, in the context of South Africa, are part of the cultural process which began with Solomon Plaatje, Charlotte Manye Maxeke, Pixley ka Isaka Seme, John Langalibalele Dube, Albert Luthuli, and many others in the early part of the twentieth century reflecting the political responsibility of the intelligentsia to the people, and continues today with many other African intellectuals in South Africa.

Their political struggle in South Africa on the intellectual level is a contribution to the developing African Political Thought, whose ultimate aim is to bring about a political and cultural unity of the African peoples in Africa within a context of democratic order. In this sense, outstanding figures like Nelson Mandela and Steve Biko share a common ground with figures like Julius Nyerere, Frantz Fanon, Samora Machel, W. E. B. Du Bois, Kwame Nkrumah and Aimé Césaire.

Bibliography

Appiah, Anthony (1992). *In My Father's House: Africa and the Philosophy of Culture*. Oxford University Press, New York.

Arnold, James (1981). *Modernism and Negritude*. Harvard University Press, Cambridge.

Balseiro, Isabel and Masilela, Ntongela (Eds.), (2003). *To Change Reels: Film and Film Culture in South Africa*. Wayne State University Press, Detroit, Michigan.

Benda, Julien (1980). *The Treason of the Intellectuals*, trans. Richard Aldington. Norton, London.

Biko, Steve (1972). "Black Consciousness and the Quest for a True Humanity." In Mokgethi Motlhabi (ed.), *Essays on Black Theology*. "Black Theology Project" of the University of Christian Movement. Johannesburg.

Biko, Steve (1978a). *I Write what I like*. A selection of his writings edited by Aelred Stubbs CR. The Bowerdean Press, London.

Biko, Steve (1978b). In *The International Defence and Aid Fund*. No. 46. London.

Brewer, Anthony (1980). *Marxist Theories of Imperialism. A critical survey*. Department of Economics, University of Bristol. Routledge & Kegan Paul, London, Boston, Melbourne and Hanley.

Cabral, Amilcar (1969). "The Weapon of Theory" in *Revolution in Guinea*. Cited by Ntongela Masilela (1994) in "Pan-Africanism or Classical African Marxism?" in *Imagining Home: Class, Culture and Nationalism in the African Diaspora*." Sidney Lawrence L. & Robin D. (Eds.) Verso. London.

Césaire, Aimé (1968a). *Return to my Native Land*, translated by John Berger and Anna Bostock with an introduction by Mazisi Kunene. Penguin Books, London.

Césaire, Aimé (1968b). *Discours Sur Le Colonialisme*, the German translation *Über Den Kolonialismus*, Trans. Monika Kind. Wagenbach, Berlin.

Chrisman, Robert and Hare, Nathan (1974). *Pan-Africanism*. The Bobbs-Merrill Company.

Du Bois, W. E. B. (1986a). *Souls of Black Folk*. Fawcet, New York.

Du Bois, W. E. B. (1986b). "The Conservation of the Races," cited in Manning Marable, *W. E. B. Du Bois: Black Radical Democrat*. Twayne Publishers, Boston.

Esedebe, Olisanwuche, cited in Chuba Okadigbo, "The Odyssey and Future of Pan-Africanism," *Africa and the World. A Quarterly Journal of African Affairs*, Vol. 1, No. 1, October 1987.

Fanon, Frantz (1967a). *The Wretched of the Earth*. Penguin Books, London.

Fanon, Frantz (1967b). *Black Skin, White Masks*. Grove Press, New York.

Fanon, Frantz (1970a). *A Dying Colonialism*. Penguin Books, London.

Fanon, Frantz (1970b). *Toward the African Revolution*. Penguin Books, London.

Fierce, Milfred C. (1993). *The Pan-African Idea in the United States 1900–1919. African-American Interest in Africa and Interaction with West Africa*. Garland Publishing Inc., New York & London.

Fonlon, Bernard (1963). "Report on the Kampala Conference" in *Présence Africaine*. Vol. 17 No. 45, First Quarterly, 1963, pp. 132–133. The essay first appeared in *Abbia cultural Review journal* based in Cameroon. Fonlon is also quoted by Ntongela Masilela in *Ezekiel Mphahlele: The Last New African Intellectu-*

al of the New African Movement. (1987: p. 12) Unpublished paper. See also Mbukeni Herbert Mnguni (2009: p. 4) *The Problem of African Literature in the European Languages: A Historical Dilemma.* Paper presented to a group of African students at Free University Berlin. June 15, 2009.

Galtung, Johan (1970). "A Structural Theory of Imperialism" in *Journal of Peace Research.* Peace Research Institute, Oslo.

Geis, Imanuel (1974). *The Pan-African Movement.* African Publishing Company, New York.

Geismar, Peter (1971). *Fanon: The Revolutionary as Prophet.* Grove Press, New York.

Gouldner, Alvin W. (1979). *The Future of Intellectuals and the Rise of the New Class.* Sebury Press, New York.

Gramsci, Antonio (1967). *The Modern Prince and Other Writings.* International Publishers. New York.

Gramsci, Antonio (2005). *The Prison Notebooks: Selections.* Trans. Quintin Hoare and Geoffrey Nowell-Smith. Lawrence and Wishart, London.

Jacoby, Russell (1987). *The Last Intellectuals: American Culture in the Age of Academe.* Basic Books, New York.

James, C. L. R. (1938). *Black Jacobins.* Secker & Warburg, London.

Joseph, Celucien (2010). "Black Identity and Culture in Senghorian Negritude." *Paper presented at the annual meeting of the 33rd Annual National Council for Black Studies, Renaissance.* Altanta, GA. http://www.allacademic.com/meta/p302497_index.html

Kunene, Mazisi (1982). *The Ancestors & the Sacred Mountain.* (See an Introduction). Heinemann, London.

Kwame, Nkrumah (1965). *Neo-Colonialism: The Last Stage of Imperialism.* First published in (1965) by Thomas Nelson & Sons Ltd. London. The book was published in USA by International Publishers in 1966.

Maclean, Ian, Montefiore, Alan, & Winch, Peter (1990). *The Political Responsibility of Intellectuals.* Cambridge University Press, Cambridge.

Mandela, Nelson (1990). *Nelson Mandela: The Struggle is my Life.* Pathfinder, New York.

Mandela, Nelson (1994). *Long Walk to Freedom.* Macdonald Purnell (Pty) Ltd, Johannesburg.

Masilela, Ntongela (1986). Unpublished paper, "Frantz Fanon: Our Contemporary Zeitgeist."

Masilela, Ntongela (1987). *The Legacy of W. E. B. Du Bois (186-1963): From Aime Cesaire to Steve Biko.* Paper presented to a group of African students at the Technical University Berlin.

Masilela, Ntongela (1994). "Pan-Africanism or Classical African Marxism?" in *Imagining Home,* Sidney Lewrence & Robin D. G. Lecey (eds.). Verso, London.

Mchunu, Vusi and Mnguni, Mbukeni Herbert (eds.) (1987). "Spirits of Steve Biko" in *Awa Finnaba. An African Literary Cultural Journal.* No. 10. Berlin.

Mnguni, Mbukeni Herbert (1986). "Winnie Madikizela Mandela and Her Struggle against Apartheid." In Vusi Mchunu and Mbukeni Herbert Mnguni (eds.), *Awa Finnaba. An African Literary Cultural Journal.* Berlin.

Mnguni, Mbukeni Herbert (1987). "African Intellectuals and the Development of African Political Thought in the Twentieth Century" in *Présence Africaine. Cultural Review of the Black World.* 161/162. Paris.

Mnguni, Mbukeni Herbert (1992). "ISouth Africa Yilizwe Elingenaso Isizwe – South Africa is a Country without a Nation" in *Ilanga lase Natal,* December 18, 1992.

Mnguni, Mbukeni Herbert (1998). *Education as a Social Institution and Ideological Process: From the Négritude Education in Senegal to a Bantu Education in South Africa.* In Christoph Wulf (ed.), European Studies in Education. Waxmann, Münster.

Mnguni, Mbukeni Herbert (2000). "Cyril Lionel Robert James and Africa" in *Présence Africaine, Cultural Review of the Black World.* Paris.

Mnguni, Mbukeni Herbert (2008). "Ukunyamalala Kwezifundiswa Ezimnyama eSouth Africa – The Disappearance of Black Intellectuals in South Africa" in *Ilanga lase Natal,* March 18, 2008.

Mnguni, Mbukeni Herbert (2009). *Ufuduko LwamaZulu Nesimanje* – (Zulu Migration and Modernity). Maskew Miller Longman Publishers, Johannesburg, South Africa.

Mondlane, Eduardo (1969). *The Struggle for Mozambique.* Penguin African Library, London.

Mphahlele, Ezekiel (1967). "Remarks on Negritude." In Ezekiel Mphahlele (ed.), *African Writing Today* (pp. 247–253). Penguin Books. See also Mphahlele, Ezekiel (1962). *The African Image.* London: Faber and Faber.

Nesbitt, Nick (2010). "Art as Affirmation; A response to Maerhofer's Poetic of Négritude in the context of Historical Avant-Garde in relation to Sartre and Value. *African writers index.*

Ngugi wa Thiong'o (1981). *Detained.* Heinemann, London.

Niger, Paul (1978). Quoted by Dr. Okpanachi in *A Song for Inikpi* (A collection of Poems) Salem University. (1990, p. 69) Lokoja. Kraft Books Ltd. See also Mnguni, Mbukeni Herbert, (1998, p. 125) *Education as a Social institution and Ideological Process: From the Negritude Education in Senegal to a Bantu Education in South Africa.* Waxmann: Münster.

Nkosi, Lewis (1983). "Literature and Liberation". In Lewis Nkosi, *Home and Exile and Other Selections*. London: Longman.

Oguejiofor, J. Obi (2009). "Negritude as Hermeneutics: A Reinterpretation of Léopold Sédar Senghor's Philosophy" in *American Catholic Philosophical Quarterly*. Volume 83. Issue 1. Winter 2009, 94.

Okadigbo, Chuba (1986). *Consciencism in African Political Philosophy* Fourth Dimension Publishers, Enugu Nigeria.

Okadigbo, Chuba (1987). "The Odyssey and Future of Pan-Africanism in Africa and the World" in *A Quarterly Journal of African Affairs*. Vol. 1. No. 1. New Frontier Publishers.

Ouologuem, Yambo (1988). *Bound to Violence* written in 1969 in French and published in English 1971. And published again in December 28th 1983 by Heinemann Educational Books. In 1988 quoted by Ezekiel Zungu in *Ouloguem Yambo's Literary Voice UmAfrika*, p. 15.

Robinson, Cedric J. (1987). "Fanon and the West: Imperialism in the Native Imagination." *Africa and the World. A Quarterly Journal of African Affairs*. Vol. 1 No. 1. New Frontier Publishers, London.

Said, Edward W. (1987). "Third World Intellectuals," *Salmagundi*, No. 74–75, October.

Said, Edward W. (1994). *Representations of the Intellectual. The 1993 Reith Lectures*. Vintage Press.

Salhi, Kamil (2004). "Rethinking Francophone Culture: African and the Caribbean between History and Theory," *Research in African Literatures*.

Sartre, Jean-Paul (1947). *Black Orpheus*. Trans. S. W. Allen, *Présence Africaine* (1971, pp. 36–39). Paris.

Sartre, Jean-Paul (1964). *Search for a Method*. London.

Sartre, Jean-Paul (1985). Preface, Frantz Fanon, *The Wretched of the Earth*. Penguin Books, London, Reprint.

Senghor, L. S. (1962). "Discours devant le parlement de Ghana."

Serequeberhan, Tsenay (1994). *The Hermeneutics of African Philosophy: Horizon and Discourse*. Routledge, London.

Shepperson, George (1960). "Notes on Negro American Influence on the Emergence of African Nationalism," *Journal of African History*, Vol. 1, No. 2.

Shils, Edward (1958). "The Intellectuals and the Powers: Some Perspectives for Comparative Analysis", *Comparative Studies in Society and History*, Vol. 1.

Soyinka, Wole (1976). *Myth, Literature, and the African World*. Cited in Nick Nesbett "Senghor-Negritude as an African Way of Life." (December 29, 2007).

Soyinka, Wole (1998). *The Burden of Memory the Muse of Forgiveness*. Published February 1st 2000. Oxford University Press, USA.

Wadlow, Rene (2006). *Leopold Sedar Senghor: "Who will teach rhythm to the world laid low by machines and cannons?"*

Washington, Paula B. (1980). "Legacy of South African Freedom Fighter". Book Review of: Biko, Steve (1978). *I Write What I Like*. In *Freedomways. A Quarterly Review of the Freedom Movement*. Vol. 20. No. 1, (1980, p. 52) New York.

Wa Thiong'o, Ngugi (1981). *Detained: A Writer's Prison Diary*. Heinemann. London. Also "Literature and Society" in *Writers in Politics*. London. See also "Mau Mau is Coming Back" in *Barrel of a Pen*. op. cit., pp. 7–31. Wa Thiong'o Ngugi, (1981b) *Detained: A Writer's Prison Diary*. Heinemann. London.

Wa Thiong'o, Ngugi (1983). "National Identity and Imperialist Domination: The Crisis of Culture in Africa Today," in *Barrel of a Gun*. New Beacon Books, London.

Woods, Donald (1978). *BIKO*. Penguin Books, London.

Part Three

African Languages: Obstacles to Internationalism or Additional Wealth for the World?

Jabulani S. Maphalala[1]

African languages are facing extinction unless African governments on the African continent pass legislations to oblige all people of African ancestry and any foreigners living in Africa to use these languages in education, commerce and government (Maphalala, 2000, p. 148). It must be borne in mind that Africa is the second largest continent in the world and that Medu Netcher—Mdw Ntr—the most ancient written African language on the continent, dating from about 3300 BCE, was, as Dr Theophile Obenga (1997, p. 37) has observed, both a language and a script. A language is a systematic structure of arbitrary vocal symbols by which members of a social group communicate (Obenga, 1997, p. 36). It has long since been established that the first civilisation was created along the Hapi (renamed Nile) river by the African people and that Kemet (ancient Egypt) was its first daughter (see Hilliard III, 1994, pp. 127–147). Thus, the civilisation that we have in the world today is the refinement of the civilisation which was created by African people on the African continent (Karenga, 1988, pp. 21–24).

Most African traditional languages on the African continent are linked to Medu Netcher. They include *isiZulu* in South Africa, Yoruba and Hausa

---

[1] Jabulani S. Maphalala, is currently working at eMandulo Consulting Agency CC. in South Africa. He received his B.A. in 1974, and his B.A. Hons. in 1975. He attained his M.A. in 1979 on the topic *The Participation of the Zulus in the Anglo-Boer War 1899–1902*, at the University of Zululand. He received his Ph.D. at the University of South Africa in History on *The Policies of the Transvaal and the Natal Governments towards Dinizulu 1897–1913*. He has taught at the University of Zululand. He has published several articles on history in national and international journals. He has also contributed chapters to books and read papers at conferences in Africa and abroad. He is the founding member of *Abelusi Bolimi LwesiZulu*, an organisation fighting for the Zulu language to become the medium of instruction in schools and universities. He is the author of *Ingonyama UZwelithini Mbongiziyozwa KaNyangayezizwe*, Umqulu 1, Kingspress, Empangeni, South Africa, 2002.

in Nigeria, Acoli in Nilotic, Banda and Ngibandi in the Central African Republic, Luganda in Uganda, Sena in Zambia, Snufo in Manianka, and, Bambana in Mali, Valaf in Senegal and many other African languages (Ajamu, 1997, p. 207). There is therefore no doubt that the indigenous African languages which predate most languages in the world are not obstacles to internationalism but additional wealth for the world.

In dealing with the gradual decline of African languages we must first look far back in history in order to find our way forward. The African continent was invaded by foreign invaders over many years. We know that the first of these invaders were the Hyksos, who came from Western Asia, today known as the Middle East, in 1600 BCE. The Greeks under Alexander the Great of Macedonia became the first European invaders to invade Kemet in 332 BCE. Also, from 640 CE onwards, the Arabs invaded Kemet and the northern part of the African continent (Diop, 1996, p. 98). These invasions by the Europeans and Arabs were succeeded by the Euro-Arab slave trade from the sixteenth century onwards which resulted in about 100 million African people being raped and murdered (Madhubuti, 1978, pp. 13–14). In 1884, the European powers agreed at the Congress of Berlin to divide Africa among themselves and colonise it. That colonisation resulted in the drawing of arbitrary colonial boundaries throughout Africa. South Africa was only emancipated politically in 1994 from colonial and Apartheid rule; there has as yet been no legislation passed through parliament enforcing the use of African languages in education, commerce and government. On the contrary, Afrikaans and English languages continue to be the media of instruction in schools from Grade 1 to higher education levels, and still enjoy their former colonial and Apartheid status in commerce and government (Maphalala, 2000, pp. 150–153).

The former colonisers are satisfied with the state of affairs in Africa and are adamant that anything else would be ungrateful and unacceptable (Diop, 1987, p. 13). The African political leaders, on the other hand, do not realise that people of African ancestry cannot be united through colonial languages because they can never experience the particular genius of their own languages (Diop, 1996, p. 35). Cheik Anta Diop (1987, p. 12) stressed this point by writing:

Linguistic unity based on a foreign language, however one may look at it, is cultural abortion. It would irremediably eventuate in the death of the authentic national culture, the end of our deeper intellectual and spiritual life and reduce us to perpetual copycats, having missed out on our historical mission in this world. Anglo-Saxon cultural, economic, social and even political hegemony would thereby be permanently guaranteed throughout Black Africa. We must remain radically opposed to any attempts at cultural assimilation coming from the outside: none is possible without opening the way to the others.

It must be emphasised that the present dilemma of the suppression of African languages affects all people of African ancestry including those living in diaspora. Thus, the main objective of the people of African ancestry must be the formation of the African world community. Dr Ernie Smith of the Charles R. Drew University of Medicine and Science in Los Angeles points out in *Bilingualism and the African American Child* that owing to their history as U. S. slave descendants of West Africa and Niger-Congo African origin, to the extent that Africans in America have been born into, reared into, and continue to live in linguistic environments that are different from the Euro-English speaking population, Africans in America do not acquire a Black dialect of English (Smith, 1995). However, predicated on an analysis of the sound system, word formation and use of grammar, Africans in America have retained a West and Niger-Congo African phonology and morpho-syntax in the substratum of their speech. Thus, based on linguistic studies and findings, African speech in America is the linguistic continuation of Africa in Black America (Smith, 1995). The same could be said of Africans living in Brazil and and for example in the Caribbean.

Thus, the independence of African states from colonial rule throughout the continent is still incomplete for three fundamental reasons caused by centuries of mental, psychological and philosophical dependence on Eurocentric values (T'shaka, 1995, p. 95). First, while education of children the world over is conducted in their mother tongue, in Africa, from Cape Town to Cairo, and in the diaspora, African children from Grade 1 to university level are taught using colonial languages: Afrikaans, English, Arabic, Portuguese, German and French. This state of affairs disconnects African people from their history (Carruthers, 1997, p. 66). There are as of yet no African primary schools, secondary schools nor African universities on the African continent. Thus, millions of African learners have to first think about the meaning of words before tackling problems in various subjects in schools, which causes six years of backwardness in the acquisition of information which they would have easily acquired was school education conducted in their home languages (Diop, 1996, pp. 35–36). Also, African children are alienated because the education they receive from these schools is Eurocentric.

The second reason why independence of African states from colonial rule is incomplete is, the languages used by governments in public, political documents and acts—parliamentary debates, for the drawing up of constitutions and legal codes, in police stations, the magistrate courts, the post offices and so on—are colonial languages. The millions of people of African ancestry at the grassroots level who cannot use these languages as effective tools find it extremely difficult to express themselves in their countries of birth and are therefore not empowered. In most parts of the world, the opposite is usually the case, the home language is used as the official public language to allow the citizens to debate effectively all the nitty gritties facing their countries. We therefore agree with Cheik Anta Diop (1987, p. 10) that using the coloniser's language is a convenient way to avoid facing the true complaints of the population, who may be illiterate but are not without good sense.

The third issue which makes the independence of all African states incomplete is that the languages that are used in commerce and industry—the languages of communication in the work place, those which are used at interviews when millions of African people apply for jobs, those which are used in producing business reports and business plans, those which appear on all manufactured goods in big and small businesses—are those of the former colonisers, which cannot be used as effective tools by millions of African people at the grassroots level. Also, commercial advertisements on television are mainly in colonial languages. We must remember that the sense of sight accounts for 75% of our knowledge (Browder, 1989, pp. 83–85). Thus, the monopoly of foreigners over television in African states has resulted in African children growing up emulating foreigners and tending to look down upon people of African ancestry and their culture.

Another primary cause of the suppression of African languages is the fact that the constitutions governing African states since their emancipation from colonial rule are based on law, which is a Eurocentric enterprise. It is well-known that European law was used in the conquest and enslavement of Africa and other native peoples (Nunn, 1997, p. 356). It has also been established that nothing was done without the Eurocentric law's guiding hand to regulate, manage and control (Nunn, ibid., pp. 352–353). Following the political emancipation of Africa from European colonial rule, Eurocentric constitutions, instead of Afrocentric constitutions, were adopted by all the newly emancipated African states including South Africa. This perpetuated the colonial status quo with disastrous consequences for the people of African ancestry and their languages. With respect to law and cultural oppression Prof. Kenneth B. Nunn (ibid., p. 363) observes that

> [l]aw is used by Eurocentric culture to infiltrate and subjugate other cultural spheres. Law's role is to legitimate European domination through its rulings and judgements. But law advances white cultural hegemony through its processes, as well as through its results. The very form that legal reasoning and legal analysis takes affirms white Eurocentric culture. Legal analysis proceeds on the assumption that it is possible to logically extract a concrete legal conclusion from objective legal principles. This requires those who would use the legal system to adopt the modalities of Eurocentric thought. An argument is simply not cognizable in legal terms unless it is objectified, rationalized and abstracted. This has two negative consequences. First it gives the impression that "arational" or subjective thought, is inferior, or at least nonfunctional. Second, problems that are not reducible to abstract formulations go unaddressed and unresolved.

The common law itself is an abstraction that results from the restatement of Anglo-Saxon customs as opinions of English courts (Nunn, ibid., p. 348). Thus, there is an urgent need in Africa to adopt Afrocentric constitutions which can be understood by millions of people of African ancestry to prevent them from languishing in overcrowded gaols in their millions and to prevent the destruction of their languages and culture.

The trend today the world over is: "think globally—act locally." In short, the foundation of nations must not be destroyed through globalisation, and multilingualism must be non-negotiable. Thus, according to Dr Kjell Herberts (1999) of the Åbo Akademi University at Vaasa-Vasa in Finland in a conference keynote address titled *Challenges from Multilingual cities—conflict or co-operation,* with 44 independent states now being part of Europe following the collapse of the Soviet Union, there are altogether 225 living languages that are supported by the European Charter for Regional or Minority Languages. Different minority languages in the same country, according to Herberts, can therefore receive different support due to demographic, social and economic circumstances.

Most importantly, argues Dr Herberts, there are different measures to promote the use of minority languages in the fields of education, law and administration, media, and culture. The Charter has been signed by 20 member states and ratified by eight members. It is, according to Dr Herberts, a useful toolbox in defining the usage of particular minority languages in a country or city. Thus, the primary concern in most developed countries of the world today is to promote all languages in education, government and commerce.

India, for many decades after its independence, used English as the official language but today, according to Prof. Omkar M. Koul (1999) of the Central Institute of Indian languages in India in *Multilingualism and Local Government in India*, the Constitution of India recognises 18 major languages. The constitution declares Hindi in Devanagri script as the official language of the Union along with English as an associate official language.

The suppression of African languages has compounded the issue of "Cultural AIDS," which has the same devastating effects upon the people of African ancestry as the AIDS virus, and will inevitably be followed by the extinction of people of African ancestry. The main reason for this is put as follows by Hilliard III (2000):

> It is natural that members of ethnic groups are able to identify members of their own family quite readily. However, when the cultural aids virus attacks,

family solidarity is weakened and in extreme conditions, may disappear altogether. When alien cultural ideas and behaviors are imbibed wholesale and uncritically, and when *the source of authority for the validity of emerging cultural forms* is outside the ethnic family, we may identify that phenomenon as cultural AIDS. The family loses its center, unable to tell friend from foe, unable to use its cultural base in framing its options. Institutional structures wither. Structures such as schools, churches, recreation, business, etc. lose any ethnic flavor. Then members of the group begin to perceive themselves merely as individuals, frequently as bit players in someone else's ethnic family. (emphasis in original)

The cultural AIDS virus has already caused untold harm in various parts of Africa. Chinweizu argues that Nigerians are no longer competent in the indigenous African languages of that country and that very few of them can speak Nigerian languages without dragging in English words and phrases for which serviceable equivalents exist in their home language. Thus, Nigerian languages as spoken by Nigerians tend to be bastardised varieties exemplified by what is derisively called "Englibo" or "Hausanchi." Chinweizu has termed this kind of bastardisation half-baked bilingualism. Those who suffer from this condition cannot effectively speak, write, read, think, feel or verbally relate to their environment in either English or their home language (Chinweizu, 1994, p. 92).

The same deplorable condition of persons who are severely handicapped and without proficiency even in one language is found throughout South Africa and popularly known as "Tsotsi Taal" or "Fanakalo." The broadcasters of u*Khozi* FM (formerly Zulu Radio Broadcasting Station), which broadcasts to about six million listeners in South Africa, Swaziland and parts of the United States, can no longer count in isiZulu despite the facts highlighted by C. Zaslavsky (1979) which provide African contribution to science and mathematics. By using numbers and patterns as organising principles, Zaslavsky describes the numeration systems all of which reveal a high understanding of mathematics. On *uKhozi* FM, all telephone numbers and area codes, weather conditions, times and months are now broadcast to millions of Zulu listeners, who are mainly illiterate and semi-illiterate, using the English language.

Regarding the area codes and telephone numbers, 100% of *uKhozi* FM radio announcers broadcast them using English. For example, the number may be (035) 7933630. All these announcers say is: the area code is zero, three, five and the number is seven, nine, double three, six, three, zero. The correct announcement in isiZulu should be: *ikhodi ithi: iqanda, okuthathu, okuhlanu. Inombolo yocingo ithi: isikhombisa, isishiyagalolunye, okuthathu nokuthathu, isithupha, okuthathu neqanda.* This would be easily understood by millions in the rural and semi-rural areas where the majority of African people live and go a long way toward keeping *isiZulu* alive because the danger is that every extinct language means that traditions, heritage, folklore, identities, and ways of thinking and living also die.

It is well known how important it is for listeners to know the times of the day for them to attend properly to their work. Most of the Zulu presenters on *uKhozi* FM use the English language to communicate the times of the day to their listeners. They will say: *isikhathi manje* (the time now is) *ngu* half past six, instead of *seligamenxe ihora lesithupha*, or *ngu* ten to seven, instead of *sekusele imizuzu elishumi kushaye ihora lesikhombisa*.

Another serious mistake by Zulu presenters of *uKhozi* FM suffering from "Cultural AIDS" is to replace Zulu months with English ones. The names of the Zulu months are part of Zulu and African heritage, and replacing them with English ones is confusing for millions of listeners and unnecessary.

The Zulu names for the months are: *Masingana* (January), *Nhlolanja* (February), *Ndasa* (March), *Mbaso* (April), *Nhlaba* (May), *Nhlangulana* (June), *Ntulikazi* (July), *Ncwaba* (August), *Mandulo* (September), *Mfumfu* (October), *Lwezi* (November), and *Zibandlela* (December).

It is already known that there are about 6 700 living languages in the world today and that 2 000, or 30%, of them are spoken in Africa. Yet, estimates suggest that in the following 30 to 40 years—in one generation—about half of them will die out. The threatened languages are mainly spoken languages without literature and institutional support such as schooling and mass media. When the author of this paper challenged these Zulu presenters in open debate on their broadcasting station, they defended their action by pointing out that the use of *isiZulu* wastes a lot of time and that *uKhozi* FM was a business undertaking. It was interesting, however, to note that most Zulu listeners who participated in the debate agreed with me and expressed their disgust about the actions of the Zulu presenters.

Another problem is the drastic decline in the number of African people who can speak colonial languages correctly. Most African teachers in African schools cannot use the colonial languages as effective tools. The result is that the subject matter which is imparted to the African learners is not informative and difficult to understand resulting in thousands of African learners failing their matriculation examinations.

Thus, the non-usage of African languages as the media of instruction in schools is a very serious issue. It is an undisputed fact that a people lives as long as its language lives in the mouth of the people. There is no violence more unbearable than that which seeks to rob a people of the heritage created by countless generations of forebears. A language once taken away can never be re-created. Once it is dead, so is the people. Ushinsky argues that language is a teacher who taught the people when there were yet no books and no schools, and will continue to teach them till the end of the people's history (Ushinsky, 1975, pp. 244–245).

As each new generation easily and without effort masters its native language, it at the same time acquires the fruits of the thoughts and feelings of thousands of preceding generations which have long since turned to dust in the native soil. Everything that these countless generations of forebears had seen, everything they had experienced, everything they had felt and pondered, is transmitted easily and without effort to the child who has only just opened his eyes to the world, and the child, having learned his native language, enters life with boundless power. It is not only conventional sounds that children get when they study their own language; they drink in spiritual life and strength from the breast of the mother tongue. It explains nature to them as no naturalist could; it acquaints them with the character of the people around them, with the society in the midst of which they live, with its history and its aspirations as no historian could;

it introduces them to folk beliefs and to the folk poetry as no aesthete could; and it gives them, finally, such logical concepts and philosophical views as, of course, no philosopher could.

The fundamental objective for people of African ancestry must be to teach their children using African languages and eventually to create an African world community. There must be African primary schools, secondary schools and universities on the African continent where the media of instruction is African languages. There must be four African indigenous languages which must be chosen and used as the general languages of the African continent, similar to French, English and German, which are the general languages of debate among Europeans on the European continent.

Cheik Anta Diop (1987, p. 11) provided a pragmatic solution to how colonial languages can be replaced with African languages in education, the workplace and government throughout the African continent. He correctly argued that in each African state there is a main African language which is spoken by the overwhelming majority of African people there. This has been the case since precolonial times. But because of the size of the African continent it may perhaps be sufficient to select four African languages as the languages of the African continent (Diop, ibid., p. 10).

According to Diop, *Valaf* in Senegal may be the main language selected to replace French in that country. Research to identify appropriate languages in other African states may be conducted along similar lines. The fundamental point is that these main languages must be developed through scientific commissions with supporting dictionaries and gradually replace colonial languages in African states in education, commerce and government. Gradually, a competent, interterritorial commission comprising African patriots must be formed to decide which four African languages are to be selected as the languages of people of African ancestry on the African continent (Diop, ibid., p. 11).

Following the decision of such a commission, all people of African ancestry must then use the selected languages as the languages of the African continent in education, commerce and government. *Colonial languages* could still be used as elective foreign languages in secondary schools but their dominance in education, the work place and government will be wiped out.

There is validity in Diop's argument because African languages are culturally united, having originated from the same world-view. The Zulu language is more different from French, English or Italian than it is from *seSotho* or *Valaf* (Diop, 1996, p. 37). Diop has also pointed out that out of the 600 languages mentioned as the languages of Africa, many are dialects and only four main languages can be regarded as the real languages of the African continent.

The solution of choosing the languages of people of African ancestry will solve the problem of African intellectuals delivering their conference papers and writing their books in colonial languages, thereby impoverishing millions of their own people. By doing this, these African intellectuals are enriching these colonial languages (Diop, 1996, p. 36) but not African languages. Thus, African intellectuals are also prisoners of the colonial languages. Finding lasting solutions is an urgent matter, to uplift millions of people of African ancestry on the African continent and in the *diaspora*.

South Africa, a country of about 1,219,090 km^2, with a population of about 40,583,573 million people, provides a convenient place where colonial languages (English and Afrikaans) can easily be replaced by an African language in education, commerce and government. The population by race in South Africa is as follows: African, 31.1 million; European, 4.4 million; Coloured, 3.6 million; Indian, 1.0 million; and unspecified groups, 0.4 million.

There are nine provinces with the following populations: the province of the Kingdom of KwaZulu, 8.4 million; Gauteng, 7.3 million; Eastern Cape, 6.3 million; Northern Province, 4.9 million; Western Cape, 4.0 million; North West, 3.4 million; Mpumalanga, 2.8 million; Free State, 2.6 million; and Northern Cape, 0.8 million. Regarding the home language in these provinces we find that *isiZulu* accounts for 9.2 million speakers; isiXhosa, 7.2 million; Afrikaans, 5.8 million; sePedi, 3.7 million; English, 3.5 million;

seTswana, 3.3 million; seSotho, 3.1 million; siTsonga, 1.8 million; siSwati, 1.0 million; siVenda, 0.9 million; isiNdebele, 0.6 million; and unspecified, 0.6 million (Statistics South Africa, 1996).

The fundamental point about these figures is that *isiZulu* is number one on the list and spoken by the overwhelming number of inhabitants—22.9% of the population of South Africa (Statistics South Africa, 1998)—and long before the colonisation of South Africa, minor language groups were able to speak *isiZulu* plus their own languages without any difficultty. Thus, in a scientific survey conducted by Markdata Strategic Research Solutions on behalf of the Pan South African Language Board (Pansalb), seven out of the nine provinces of South Africa stressed that they preferred *isiZulu* as the official language of the country (Pansalb, 2000, pp. 1–27). Also, *isiZulu* is currently spoken as the home language by the overwhelming majority in the most populous and rich province of Gauteng—about 21,5% of the population—and in the Mpumalanga province Zulu speakers are also in the majority making up 25.4% of the population. In the province of the Kingdom of KwaZulu, Zulu speakers make up 79.8% of the population.

We also know that the Zulu language transcends the colonial borders of South Africa since about 20% of Zulu descendants, known as the amaNdebele, live in Zimbabwe, and a sizeable number in southern Mozambique, southern Tanzania, Malawi and Zambia. These peoples are linked to the Zulu language for historical reasons (Maphalala, 2000, pp. 149–151). This means that the Southern Africa Development Countries (SADC) can easily replace English as their language of debate with *isiZulu* with much greater benefits for people of African ancestry at the grassroots level. But be it as it may, the whole task of deciding which African languages are to replace colonial languages on the African continent can best be done by a competent interterritorial commission of African patriots.

Bibliography

Ajamu, Adisa (1997). "From Tef Tef to Medew Nefer. The importance of Utilization of African Languages. Terminologies, and Concepts in the Rescue, Restoration, Reconstruction, and Reconnection of African Ancestral memory," in Carruthers and Leon Harris, (eds.), *African World Project.*

Browder, Anthony (1989). *From the Browder File. 22 Essays on the African American Experience.* Washington: The Institute of Karmic Guidance.

Carruthers, Jacob (1997). "An African Historiography for the 21st Century, in Carruthers and Leon Harris, (eds.), *African World Project, The Preliminary Challenge.* Los Angeles: ASCAC, pp. 47–72.

Chinweizu, Ibekwe (1994). "Toward a Black Language policy: the Nigerian case," *Black Renaissance* 1(1) January: 87–100.

Deprez, Kas (2000). "Public Policy and African Languages, The Case of isiZulu." In Deprez and Theo du Plessis (eds.), *Studies in Language Policy in South Africa, Multilingualism and Government, Belgium, Luxembourg, Switzerland, Former Yugoslavia and South Africa.* Pretoria: Van Schaik Publishers.

Diop, Cheik (1987). *Black Africa. The Economic and Cultural Basis for a Federated State.* Trenton: Africa World Press.

Diop, Cheik (1996). *Towards the African Renaissance. Essays in Culture and Development 1946–1960.* London: Karnak House.

Herberts, Kjell (1999). *Challenges from Multilingual Cities – Conflict or Co-Operation.* Keynote Address read at a Conference on "Multilingual Cities and Towns in South Africa-Challenges and Prospects." CSIR Conference Centre, Pretoria, Manuscript.

Hilliard III, Asa (1994). "Bringing Maat, Destroying Isfet: The African and African Diasporan presence in the Study of Ancient KMT," in Ivan Van Sertima, (ed.), *Egypt, Child of Africa.* New Brunswick, Transaction Publishers, pp. 127–147.

Hilliard III, Asa (2000). *Cultural Aids: The scourge of the African World.* University of Georgia, USA, Manuscript.

Karenga, Maulana (1988). "The Meaning and Challenge of African History," in Addai-Sebo and Ansel Wong, (eds.), *Our Story. A Handbook of African History and Contemporary Issues.* London: Strategic Policy Unit, pp. 11–28.

Koul, Omkar (1999). *Multilingualism and Local Government in India.* Paper read at a conference on "Multilingual Cities and Towns in South Africa – Challenges and Prospects." CSIR Conference Centre, Pretoria, Manuscript.

Madhubuti, Haki (1978). *Enemies: The Clash of Races.* Chicago: Third World Press.

Maphalala, Jabulani (2000). *The Zulus and the Boer War.* Reviewed in *History Today.* Vol. 50. No. 1. Also by Jabulani, Maphalala, "KwaZulu Natal is not an English Colony." *Natal Mercury.* (3 November 1999). And "Pure Zulu faces a new invasion." *Natal Mercury.*

Nunn, Kennet (1997). "Law as a Eurocentric Enterprise." *Law and Equality, Journal of Theory and Practice,* 15[2] Spring: 323–371.

Obenga, Theophile (1997). "Who Am I? Interpretation in African Historiography," in Carruthers and Leon Harris, (eds.), *African World project. The Preliminary Challenge*. Los Angeles, ASCAC, pp. 31–44.

Pan South African Language Board (2000). Report on "Language Use and Language Interaction in South Africa. A National Socio-linguistic Survey conducted by Markdata on behalf of Pansalb, December.

Smith, Ernie (1995). *Bilingualism and the African American Child. A Seminar presented at The Language Development Program for the African American Students – Weekend Staff Development Conference, Charles R. Drew University of Medicine and Science*. Los Angeles, 13 May, Manuscript.

Statistics South Africa (1996). Mary Alexander at marya@mediaclubsouthafrica.com

Statistics South Africa (1998). Mary Alexander at marya@mediaclubsouthafrica.com

T'shaka, Oba (1995). *Return to the African Mother Principle of Male and Female Equality, Vol. I*. Oakland: Pan Afrikan Publishers and Distributers.

Ushinsky, K. (1975). *Selected Works*. Moscow: Progress Publishers.

Zaslavsky, Claude (1979). *Africa Counts, Number and Pattern in African Culture*. Connecticut: Lawrence Hill and Company.

Index

Abantu Abamnyama 41, 42
Abantu-Batho 25, 26, 52, 86
Abdurahman, Abdullah 102
Abrahams, Peter 85–87, 90, 109
Acoli 144; *see also* language (traditional)
Africa (continent) 9–22, 25–33, 36, 38, 39, 43, 44, 46, 47, 51, 53–55, 58, 60, 61, 65–67, 70–72, 74, 75, 77, 81, 82, 84, 86–91, 93, 94, 96–98, 100–109, 111, 113–122, 124, 125, 126, 129–137, 143–145, 147, 149, 150, 153, 154
African Americans 38, 40, 44, 101; *see also* Black Americans
African-American intellectuals 116
African intellectuals; *see* New African intellectuals
African languages 19, 20, 23, 143–145, 147–149; *see also* language (traditional)
African Marxism 16, 113; *see also* Marxism
African Methodist Episcopal Church 29, 56
African National Congress (ANC) 18, 26, 28, 43, 45, 47–49, 52, 56, 57, 60–65, 69, 73–78, 83, 85, 86, 92, 96, 100, 102, 104, 106, 113, 134–136
    ANC Youth League 49, 52, 56, 64, 73, 76, 78, 102
    President-General 45, 47, 52, 65, 69, 77, 78, 83, 85
    Programme of Action 47, 76, 85
African nationalism 83, 123; *see also* nationalism
African socialism 17; *see also* socialism

Afrikaans 42, 144, 145, 153
Afrikaner 49, 73, 76, 79, 80
Afrikaner Nationalism 49, 73, 76, 79, 80; *see also* nationalism
Aggrey, James Emman Kwegyir 30, 31, 41
AIDS 20, 148–150
    "cultural AIDS" 20, 149
Ajamu, Adisa 144
Alexander the Great 144
Algeria
    Algerian Revolution 127–129
"Amicus Homini Gentis" 25, 35, 55
Anderson, Mariam 57
Anglo-Boer War 61, 143
apartheid 78, 79, 86, 134, 136
Arendt, Hannah 127, 128
Armstrong, Louis 14, 57
Arusha Declaration (1967) 132
assimilation 16, 114, 123, 145
Atlantic Charter 117
Azikiwe, Mnandi 57, 117
Bacon, Francis 34, 97
Balkema, A.A. 38
Bambana 144; *see also* language (traditional)
Bambatha Rebellion 107
Banda 144; *see also* language (traditional)
Bantu 13, 14, 26, 27, 30, 32–34, 39, 42, 50–54, 56–58, 61–75, 78, 80, 81, 83, 85, 86, 90, 92, 93, 95, 99–102, 106, 108, 111, 133
Bantu Men's Social Centre 46
Bantu World 13, 32, 48, 50, 51, 57, 62, 63, 66, 68, 85, 86, 90, 101, 108
Basotho 32

Biko, Steve 16, 18, 113, 133–137
Black Americans 12–14, 22; *see also* African Americans
Black Community Programmes 134
Black Consciousness Movement, (BCM) 113, 134
Black Diaspora 10, 11, 21
Black, Stephen 50
Blyden, Edward Wilmot 30, 116, 117
Bokwe, John Knox 29, 59, 99
Botha, Louis 32
Brazil 19, 145
British Empire 26, 33, 58, 60, 71, 104, 106, 117, 123; *see also* England
British Labour Movement 104
British South Africa 33
Bud-M'Belle, Isaac 41, 57, 102
Cabral, Amilcar 17, 18, 58, 112, 115, 120, 127, 128, 130, 133
Cairo (Egypt) 145
Caluza, Rueben 39, 44, 57
Cambridge University 34
Cape Town (South Africa) 28, 38, 106, 145
Caribbean 19, 145
Carlyle, Thomas 42, 43
Carruthers, Jacob 145
Carter-Karis Collection 47, 71, 73
Catholicism 31, 34, 36
Central African Republic 144
Césaire, Aimé 10, 16, 21, 112, 115, 121, 122, 126, 133, 136, 137
Champion, A. G. W. 32, 47, 49, 57, 72, 73, 77–79, 89, 103, 107, 108
Chicago, IL (United States) 26, 27, 73
Chinweizu 149
Christianity 11, 34, 37, 40, 48, 49, 53, 59, 75, 95, 97, 98, 104, 134
civilization 19, 37, 38, 111

colonialism 10, 15–18, 21, 23, 75, 112, 114, 115, 117–119, 121, 126–128, 130
Columbia University 15, 100
Commonwealth (Institution) 119
communism 73, 105
Congo 118, 132, 145
  Congo Crisis (1960–1961) 118, 132
Congress of South African Writers 94
Congress of the People 137
Constantine, Learie 57
Cope, A.T. 41
Cressy, Harold 103
Cromwell, Alexander 100, 109
Cuba
  Cuban revolution 128
"cultural AIDS" 20, 149
Damas, Leon 115, 121
Dar es Salaam 119
de Chardin, Teilhard 126
declaration; *see also* Arusha Declaration
Defiance Campaign (South Africa, 1952) 53, 86, 135
Delany, Martin 15, 100, 109
Dhlomo, Herbert Isaac Ernest 11, 14, 26, 30–33, 35–40, 42, 43, 45–52, 54, 55, 63, 65, 66, 68–72, 77, 78, 81, 82, 84, 85, 87, 89, 91–96, 101, 102, 107, 108
Dhlomo, R. R. R. 11, 32, 35, 39, 42, 43, 48, 50, 51, 57, 66, 70, 90, 93, 101–103, 105
Diagne, Blaise 16, 114, 115
Dingane 50
Diop, Birago 121
Diop, Cheik 144, 146, 152, 153
Drew, Charles 14, 57, 145
Drum 7, 13, 23, 25, 32–34, 51, 57, 66, 72, 83–85, 87–91, 93, 95, 108

Dube, John Langalibalele 11–14, 18, 28, 29, 31, 32, 38–41, 43, 44, 46, 57, 62, 66, 69, 69–71, 75–77, 96, 100, 102, 108, 137
    Insila ka Shaka 38
Du Bois, W. E. B. 12, 13–16, 29, 42, 43, 57, 66, 87, 96, 101, 108, 111, 112, 116, 134, 137
Durban 41, 48, 134
Dwane, James 99
Eastern Cape (province in South Africa) 153
education 9, 11, 13, 20, 26, 27, 29, 34, 35, 39, 40, 46, 61, 69, 71, 77, 88, 89, 91, 95, 98, 104, 143–146, 148, 152, 153
Egypt 143
Ellington, Duke 57
England 28, 86, 89, 111, 116
    London 10, 27, 29, 86, 87, 88, 95, 96
English language 25, 35, 39, 45, 61, 80, 97, 100, 102, 124, 144, 145, 148–150, 152–154
Europe 9, 11, 12–14, 19, 22, 36, 53, 54, 56, 58, 60, 63, 64, 75, 89, 91, 92, 94, 98, 99, 111, 112, 115, 117, 123–126, 128, 129, 132, 144, 147, 148, 152, 153
    European Charter 148
Existentialism 125, 129
Fanakalo 149; *see also* Tsotsi, W.M.
Fanon, Frantz 10, 16–18, 21, 112, 114, 115, 120, 125–131, 133, 137
First, Ruth 92
Fonlon, Bernard 124
Fort Hare University 30, 34, 92
France 114, 115, 123–126, 145, 152, 153
    French colonialism 115, 127
    French National Assembly 114
Francophone (Institution) 119
freedom 18, 20, 47, 54, 55, 60, 117, 135

Freedom Charter 137
Free State (province in South Africa) 153
Frobenius 126
Fuze, Magema M. 37, 40–43
Gandhi, Mohty Mahatma 102
Garvey, Marcus 16, 113, 116
Gauteng (province in South Africa) 153, 154
Ghana 17, 117
Gish, Steven D. 46, 52
Gool, Goolam H. 108
Gosani, Bob 90, 109
gospel 37
Gqoba, William Wellington 82, 98, 99
Gramsci, Antonio 113, 114, 130
Haiti
    Haitian Revolution 107
Hampton, Lionel 57
Hannibal 41
Hausa 143; *see also* language (traditional)
Hayes, Roland 57
Head, Bessie 109
Hebrew 26
Herberts, Kjell 148
Hilliard III, Asa 143, 148
Hintsa 58, 60; *see also* Xhosa
Holiday, Billie 57
Hughes, Langston 13, 45, 87
Ilanga lase Natal 13, 15, 25, 31–34, 36, 39–41, 43, 47–55, 62, 63, 65, 66, 68–72, 76, 78, 80, 87–89, 92, 93, 95, 96, 100, 101, 105
imperialism 9, 15, 16, 18, 21, 58, 60, 71, 75, 112, 114–117, 119–121, 128, 130
Imvo Zabantsundu 7, 23, 25, 26, 51, 57, 63, 97–99

159

Industrial and Commercial Workers Union of South Africa 106
Inkundla ya Bantu 13, 26, 32, 47, 51, 52, 54, 56, 58, 61–67, 69–74, 78, 80, 81, 83, 95, 101, 102
isiNdebele 154; *see also* language (traditional)
isiXhosa 153; *see also* language (traditional)
isiZulu 143, 153, 154; *see also* language (traditional)
Jabavu, Davidson Don Tengo 60–62, 103
Jabavu, John Tengo 51, 57, 61, 62, 91, 97–99
Jabavu, Noni 57
James, C. L. R. 16, 107, 113, 116, 136
Johannesburg (South Africa) 35, 46, 48, 79, 84, 91, 111
Johnson, James Weldon 14, 38, 66, 87, 94
Jordan, Archibald Campbell 11, 26, 31, 32, 36, 39, 40, 47, 49–52, 54, 56, 59, 62, 63, 65, 67–74, 76–86, 89, 90, 95, 96, 101–103, 107, 108
Joseph, Celucien 126
Joseph, Helen 92, 103
Kadalie, Clements 57, 62, 77, 78, 89, 90, 103–107
Kaffir 37, 38
Kaffirland 37
Karenga, Maulana 143
Kathrada, Ahmed Mohamed 108
Kemet 143, 144
Khaketla, Bennet Makalo 103
Khama 41
Killie Campbell African Library 41
Kotane, Moses M. 107
Koul, Omkar 148
Kumalo, L.L. 40

Kumalo, Martin K.E. 40, 70
Kunene, Mazisi 37, 112
Kuzwayo, Ellen 92, 103
KwaZulu (province in South Africa) 153, 154
language (traditional) 19, 20, 38, 39, 41, 42, 55, 118, 119, 143, 146, 149; *see also* Acoli; *see also* Bambana; *see also* Banda; *see also* Hausa; *see also* isiZulu; *see also* Luganda; *see also* Ngibandi; *see also* Sena; *see also* Snufo; *see also* Valaf; *see also* Yoruba
Lembede, Anton 32, 39, 73, 85, 90, 96, 101, 102, 103, 107
Likhing, Rev. S. J. 57
Lobengula, Chief 32
London (England) 10, 27, 29, 86–92, 95, 96
Louis, Joe 57
Luganda 144; *see also* language (traditional)
Lugg, C.H. 41
Luthuli, Albert 11, 16, 18, 31, 32, 46–49, 72, 73, 76–78, 84, 89, 103, 113, 137
Luthuli, Ngazana 32, 62, 66, 70–72
Mabaso, C.S. 57
Macaulay, Thomas 94, 98
Machel, Samora 118, 137
Madhubuti, Haki 144
Madikizela-Mandela, Winnie 92
Mafukuzela 40
Magubane 90, 107, 109
Magubane, Peter 31
Mahabane, Z.R. 57
Maimane, Arthur 89, 90, 109
Makeba, Miriam 110
Makiwane, Elijah 57, 97–99
Malan, Daniel Francois 32
Mali 144

Manchester Congress (also Pan-African Congress of 1945) 17, 116, 117, 119
Mandela, Nelson 16, 18, 81, 85, 92, 96, 103, 113, 133–137
Mangena, Alfred 26, 29, 77, 102
Manianka 144
Mapikela, T.M. 57
Mapumulo, Josiah 36, 55, 70
Marabastad (Pretoria) 91
Marxism 16, 17, 49, 73, 96, 103, 105–107, 113, 115, 128–133
Masikela, Hugh 110
Masilela, Ntongela 7, 11, 12, 14, 15, 18, 19, 23, 25, 93, 118, 124, 125, 128, 135
Masinga, K.E. 40
Matebeles 58
Matshikiza, Todd 93
Matthews, Zachariah Keodirelang 26, 49, 57, 87, 88, 103
Maxeke, Charlotte Manye 11, 12, 14, 91, 96, 102, 137
Mazingi, A.Z. 57
Mbeki, Govan 56, 58–60, 62, 102, 107
Mbuyazi 31
McKinley Roosevelt University 27
Mda, A.P. 32, 39, 72, 73, 84, 85, 90, 96, 98, 101, 103
Memmi, Albert 10, 16, 18, 21
Mhudi, Plaatje 58–60
Milton, John 34, 97
Mitsioloa, Griffiths 57
Mjamba, Harry 62
Mkize, Victor 57, 93
Mnguni, Mbukeni Herbert 3, 7, 15–19, 23, 111, 112, 122, 126, 129, 134
modernity 10–15, 18, 21, 22, 26, 27, 29, 34–46, 48–52, 56, 58–60, 66, 68–71, 74–77, 79, 82–86, 88–98, 100, 101, 104, 105, 108, 109, 111, 119, 125

Modisane, William "Bloke" 93, 109
Moeketsi, Kippie 110
Mofolo, Thomas 38, 59, 94, 102
Mokone, Mangane Maake 29, 99
Molema, Silas Modiri 77, 98, 103
Mondlane, Eduardo 16, 17, 27, 112, 127
Moroka, James 47, 76
Moshweshwe, King 32
Motsieloa, Emily 92
Mozambique 27, 154
Mpande 50
Mphahlele, Ezekiel 11, 26, 81–83, 91, 92, 95, 109, 122–124
Mphahlele, Moses 57
Mphahlele, Rebecca 92
Mpumalanga (province in South Africa) 153, 154
Mqhayi, Samuel Edward Krune 31, 38, 44, 57, 61, 81, 82, 102
Msimang, Henry Selby 11, 14, 30, 39, 57, 70, 101, 103
Msimang, Richard W. 26, 28, 29, 39, 77, 103
Mtimkulu, Don G.S. 11, 85, 88
Myeza, Theodore 43
Mzimba, Pambani Jeremiah 97, 99
Naicker, Monty G.M. 103, 107
Naidoo, G.R. 109
Nakasa, Nathaniel 109
Naransamy, Gopal 109
nationalism 13, 43, 68, 74, 76, 78–81, 83, 86, 106, 117, 123
Native Affairs Department 28
Ndebeles 32, 58
Négritude movement 125, 126
Negro Americans 38
New Africans 11, 12, 14, 15, 23, 25, 28–35, 37–40, 43–54, 56, 57, 61, 62, 64, 65, 67, 68, 70–72, 77, 79, 81, 83–85, 87–93, 99–102, 104, 105, 108

New African intellectuals 30, 31, 33, 37–40, 43, 45, 46, 50, 51, 56, 57, 61, 62, 64, 65, 67, 68, 70–72, 77, 81, 83, 88, 89, 92, 104, 105
New African Movement 28, 39, 79, 93
New African Renaissance 12, 15, 33, 93, 99–101, 104, 108
New Negroes 12, 13, 15, 44–46, 53, 57, 66, 67, 87, 88, 90, 93, 100, 101, 104, 108
New Negro intelligentsia 46
New Negro modernism 12, 15
New World Negroes 15
Ngibandi 144; *see also* language (traditional)
Ngidi, Rev. Dr. A. H. 25, 35, 36, 42, 43, 55
Ngoyi, Lilian 92, 103
Ngubane, Jordan K. 11, 26, 31, 32, 39, 40, 47, 49–52, 54, 56, 62, 63, 65–74, 76–86, 89, 90, 95, 96, 101–103, 107, 108
Nhlapo, Jacob M. 26, 55, 56, 103
Nhlapo, Walter M.B. 37, 55
Nigeria 9, 91, 144, 149
Nkosi, Lewis 90, 109, 123, 124
Nkrumah, Kwame 10, 16–18, 21, 57, 112, 115–118, 127, 132–134, 137
Northern Cape (province in South Africa) 153
Northern Province (province in South Africa) 153
North West (province in South Africa) 153
Ntantala, Phyllis 103
Ntsikana, William Kobe 58, 59, 99
Nunn, Kenneth 147

Nxumalo, Henry 11, 51, 57, 66, 85–88, 90, 93, 108, 109
Nyerere, Julius 10, 16–18, 21, 113, 118, 131, 132, 137
Nzula, Albert 14, 57, 96, 105–107
Obenga, Theophile 143
Oberlin College 12
Ohlange Institute 13, 28, 39, 69, 70, 76, 88, 96, 100, 108
Okadigbo, Chuba 117, 120
Oostendorp, Lionel 109
Oxford University 31, 34
Pan-African Congress (1925) 116, 117, 119
Pan-Africanism 9, 11, 15–19, 21, 29, 100, 107, 111, 112, 113, 115–120, 131, 132, 136
Pelem, Meshach 99
Peregrino, Francis Zaccheus Santiago 29, 51, 56, 100, 102, 104
Phelps Stokes Education Commission 30
philosophy 13, 20, 44, 52, 54, 61, 64, 74, 76, 81, 82, 88, 105, 113, 115, 118, 120, 122, 123, 125–127, 129–131, 145, 152
Plaatje, Solomon T. 11, 13, 14, 26, 30, 32, 33, 37–39, 50, 51, 57, 58, 60, 68, 70, 71, 84, 85, 93, 95, 96, 100–102, 137
poetry 34, 36, 42, 45, 55, 79, 80, 82, 122–125, 152
Pretoria (South Africa) 91
Programme of Action 47, 76, 85; *see also* African National Congress (ANC)
Protestantism 34
Radebe, Mark S. 75, 93, 98, 103
Randolph, A. Philip 90, 104
Rathebe, Dolly 93, 110

Index

rebellion 99, 114; *see also* Bambatha Rebellion
regimentation 44
revolution 17, 73, 74, 88, 106, 118, 119, 127–129
Rezant, Peter 103
Rubusana, Walter 11, 13, 26–28, 39, 50, 61, 79, 81, 84, 95, 97, 99, 100, 102
Said, Edward W. 10, 21
Sartre, Jean-Paul 118, 125, 126, 129
Schadeberg, Jurgen 109
Sekoto, Gerard 57
Seme, Pixley ka Isaka 11, 13–15, 26–29, 32, 46, 57, 62, 70, 72, 74–77, 81, 83–86, 96, 100, 103, 108, 137
Sena 144; *see also* language (traditional)
Senegal 16, 111, 144, 152
Senghor, Leopold Sedar 16, 113, 115, 121–123, 125, 126
sePedi 153; *see also* language (traditional)
seSotho 153, 154; *see also* language (traditional)
seTswana 154; *see also* language (traditional)
Shaka (also Great Shaka) 31, 38, 41, 50, 58–60, 69
Shakespeare, William 34, 97
Sharpeville Massacre (1960) 49, 51, 73, 76, 79, 109
Shelley, Percy Bysshe 31, 34
Shembe 38; *see also* Dube, John
Sisulu, Walter 103
siSwati 154; *see also* language (traditional)
siTsonga 154; *see also* language (traditional)
siVenda 154; *see also* language (traditional)
Sjambok 50
Skota, T.D. 57, 84
Smith, Ernie 145
Snufo 144; *see also* language (traditional)
socialism 17, 106, 131, 132
Soga, Allan Kirkland 13, 29, 50, 54, 71, 90, 95, 99–102, 104
Soga, Tiyo 11, 12, 14, 27, 34, 37, 38, 40, 82, 94–98
Soga, W. Z. 99
Sophiatown Renaissance 12, 14, 15, 33, 81, 83–85, 88, 89, 92–94, 102, 108, 109
South Africa
   Cape Town 28, 38, 106, 145
   Eastern Cape (province) 153
   Free State (province) 153
   Gauteng (province) 153, 154
   Industrial and Commercial Workers Union of South Africa 61, 77, 103, 106
   Johannesburg 35, 46, 48, 79, 84, 91, 111
   KwaZulu (province) 153, 154
   Mpumalanga (province) 153, 154
   Native Congress of South Africa 27, 76
   Northern Cape (province) 153
   Northern Province (province) 153
   North West (province) 153
   Pretoria 91
   South African Christian Council 48
   South African Library 28
   Tembuland 27

Transvaal (province) 28, 72, 107, 143
Union of South Africa 27, 61, 103
Western Cape (province) 153
South African Spectator 29, 51, 56, 57, 100
Staffrider Literary Generation 12, 94
Tabata, Isaac Bangani 107
Tambo, Oliver 16, 85, 103, 113
Tembuland (South Africa) 27
Thema, Richard Victor Selope 11, 13–15, 26, 30, 32, 39, 48, 50, 51, 57, 62, 63, 65–69, 71, 83–86, 90, 93–95, 101, 103, 108
Themba, Can 89–91, 93, 109
Touré, Sékou 17, 119, 120, 127
tradition 12, 14, 16, 18, 22, 27, 31, 36–40, 42, 43, 44, 50, 51, 53–58, 60, 61, 69, 70, 81–83, 85, 89, 94–97, 101, 107, 113, 114, 119, 123, 130, 133, 135, 143
Transvaal Province (South Africa) 28
"Tsotsi Taal" 149
Tsotsi, W.M. 60–62, 149
Tuskegee Institute 13, 45, 100, 108
Uganda 144
United States 26, 29, 53, 67, 69, 77, 88, 93, 100, 101, 111, 115, 116, 149
University of Witwatersrand 35, 42, 92
Ushinsky, K. 151
Valaf 144, 152, 153; *see also* language (traditional)
Verwoed, Henrik 47, 48
Vilakazi, Bambatha Benedict Wallet 25, 31–40, 42, 43, 45, 50, 55, 70, 72, 79–82, 101–103, 108

war 73, 127; *see also* Anglo-Boer War
Washington, Booker T. 12–15, 44–46, 57, 67, 69, 76, 94, 98, 100, 104, 108, 134
Waters, Ethel 57
Wauchope, Isaac W. 99
Western Cape (province in South Africa) 153
Williams, Donovan 38, 95, 97
Williams, Sylvester 29
Wright, Richard 15, 109
Xhosa 12, 27, 34, 37, 58–61, 74, 81, 94, 95, 97, 98, 100
  Hintsa 58, 60
  Xhosa Cultural Renaissance 12, 34, 37, 94, 97, 98
Xiniwe, Paul 99
Xuma, Alfred B. 11, 13, 45–47, 52, 65, 70, 77, 85, 89, 91
Yoruba 143; *see also* language (traditional)
Zambia 144, 154
Zaslavsky, Claude 149
Zulu 34, 35, 36, 38, 39, 41–43, 47, 50, 58, 72, 74, 79–81, 101, 102, 108, 111, 143, 149–151, 153, 154
  Zulu Cultural Society 47
  Zulu language 38, 41, 42, 143, 153, 154
  Zulu Nation 42
  Zulu nationalism 43